Using Rubrics to Improve Student Writing

Grade 5

REVISED EDITION

Sally Hampton

Sandra Murphy

Margaret Lowry

The International Reading Association attempts, through its publications, to provide a forum for a wide spectrum of opinions on reading. This policy permits divergent viewpoints without implying the endorsement of the Association.

Executive Editor, Books	Corinne M. Mooney
Developmental Editor	Charlene M. Nichols
Developmental Editor	Tori Mello Bachman
Developmental Editor	Stacey L. Reid
Editorial Production Manager	Shannon T. Fortner
Design and Composition Manager	Anette Schuetz
Design and Production	Progressive Information Technologies

Cover photos: (top) R. Lynn Swanson, (others) © 2008 Jupiterimages Corporation

The publisher would appreciate notification where errors occur so that they may be corrected in subsequent printings or editions.

Library of Congress Cataloging-in-Publication Data

Hampton, Sally.
Using rubrics to improve student writing, grade 5 / Sally Hampton, Sandra Murphy, Margaret Lowry. — Rev. ed.
p. cm.
Includes bibliographical references.
ISBN 978-0-87207-775-1
1. English language—Composition and exercises—Study and teaching (Elementary)—United States—Evaluation. 2. Fifth grade (Education)—United States—Evaluation. I. Murphy, Sandra. II. Lowry, Margaret. III. Title.
LB1576.H233176 2009
372.62'3044—dc22

2008030340

About the Authors

Sally Hampton is a Senior Fellow for America's Choice, Inc. Previously she served as Senior Scholar at the Carnegie Foundation for the Advancement of Teaching and as the Director of English Language Arts and Deputy Director of Research and Development for New Standards. She has taught in both urban and rural classrooms and developed reading and writing programs. Most recently she worked with Lauren Resnick to produce *Reading and Writing With Understanding*, a volume that addresses comprehension and composing in grades 4 and 5.

Sandra Murphy is a Professor Emerita at the University of California, Davis. She is interested particularly in writing assessment and its impact on teachers and curriculum, reading comprehension, and critical perspectives on literacy.

Margaret Lowry is the Director of First-Year English at the University of Texas at Arlington. She teaches courses in writing and U.S. literature and participates in the training of graduate teaching assistants. Her research interests include composition pedagogies, teacher training, and women's autobiographical writings.

About New Standards®

New Standards is a joint project of the Learning Research and Development Center at the University of Pittsburgh (Pennsylvania, USA) and The National Center on Education and the Economy (Washington, D.C., USA). From its beginning in 1991, New Standards was a leader in standards-based reform efforts. New Standards, heading a consortium of 26 U.S. states and 6 school districts, developed the New Standards® Performance Standards, a set of internationally competitive performance standards in English language arts, mathematics, science, and applied learning in grades 4, 8, and 10. New Standards also pioneered standards-based performance assessment, developing the New Standards® reference examinations and a portfolio assessment system to measure student achievement against the performance standards.

With support from the U.S. Department of Education, New Standards produced a collection of publications addressing literacy development, including the award-winning *Reading and Writing Grade by Grade*, as well as *Reading and Writing With Understanding*, *Speaking and Listening for Preschool Through Third Grade*, and a series on *Using Rubrics to Improve Student Writing* for kindergarten through fifth grade.

Writing is hard work, and teaching children to write well is very hard work. Your commitment to this challenge is vital to the future success of all the students you teach, both while they are in school and later, when they become active members of their communities.

This book provides tools to help you teach writing. It contains information about written genres and specialized rubrics that emphasize writing strategies. It also includes a collection of student work with commentaries that explain the strengths and weaknesses of the examples.

Not all the student writing in this book is at standard. Instead, we have provided you with samples that are spread out along a continuum of performance, from work that is exceptional to work that falls considerably below what children at this grade level should be expected to produce. This continuum will allow you to identify similar performances from your students and let you see how far from—or close to—standard they are. The rubrics and commentaries have been designed to provide a formative assessment to help you plan instruction.

The students whose work is included here were fortunate to have been taught by dedicated professionals like you, teachers who helped them write with exuberance and purpose about what they knew, what they thought, and what they wondered. They are novice writers, to be sure, but their potential is obvious in their ability to employ writing strategies and techniques to communicate with their audience.

We can all be guided and inspired by the work that follows.

Lauren B. Resnick
Codirector, New Standards
University of Pittsburgh

Marc S. Tucker
Codirector, New Standards
The National Center on Education and the Economy

Acknowledgments

The rubrics, student writing, and commentaries contained in this document were all compiled during the 2001–2002 school year. They were the result of work done in kindergarten through fifth-grade classrooms that used the New Standards® performance standards, the New Standards® Primary Literacy Standards, and America's Choice author and genre studies.

I would like to thank the many students, teachers, literacy coaches, and principals for their contribution to this document. The New Standards project acknowledges the work of the Noyce Foundation in the development of the rubrics.

Sally Hampton
Senior Fellow for Literacy
America's Choice, Inc.

Introduction

Formative Assessment in the Age of Accountability

In today's world, schools are being held accountable for student performance on state tests. Summative assessments of this kind provide useful information to the public and to policymakers. But the information they provide is of limited use to teachers, primarily because state assessment results arrive too late to effectively inform instruction. In this book we hope to help teachers develop an informed perspective about formative assessment and how that kind of assessment is an effective tool for instruction that fosters student learning.

There are clear differences between formative and summative assessments. Summative assessments sum up learning. They evaluate student performances in terms of where students are expected to be at the end of an instructional year or grading period.

Formative assessments, on the other hand, are intended to provide feedback and to guide instruction. Teachers who conduct formative assessments gather information about what their students know and are able to do at various points in time; using this information, they make decisions about what students need help with next. They also use this information to provide feedback to students. The best formative assessments, according to Paul Black and his colleagues, are those that provide effective feedback (see, for example, Black & Wiliam, 1998). Black describes the characteristics of such feedback as follows: First, effective feedback must be intelligible so that students can grasp its significance and use it both as a self-assessment tool and as a guide for improvement. Second, effective feedback must focus on particular qualities of the student's work. Third, effective feedback must provide advice about how to improve the work and set an achievable target. To these criteria we would add two caveats: First, effective feedback must evolve as students acquire new skills. Second, effective feedback about writing should not be generic; it should refer to particular genres and the elements and strategies associated with them.

Learning About Genres

A genre is a rough template for accomplishing a particular purpose with language. It provides the writer and the reader with a common set of assumptions about what characterizes the text. So, for example, if the text is labeled a mystery story, there is an assumption that the story line will be built around some puzzle to be resolved or some crime to be solved. Likewise, when a piece starts off "Once upon a time...," there is an assumption that we will be reading or writing a fairy tale or a parody of a fairy tale. But if the first line of a text is "Whales are mammals," we expect a very different genre—a report of information instead of a story.

As Charles Cooper (1999) explains, writers shape texts to accomplish different purposes by using and adapting particular patterns of organization, by using particular techniques to develop the text, and by making particular language choices. Although there is a lot of variation from one text to another within the same genre, texts in a particular genre nevertheless follow a general pattern. As a result, readers develop expectations that enable them to anticipate where a text is going so they can make sense of it as they read. Writers know how to order and present thoughts in language patterns readers can recognize and follow.

Lack of genre knowledge will impair a student's academic success. The student who is required to produce a report but who does not know the expectations relative to report writing is immediately disadvantaged. That student must guess at how information might be ordered, what kind of stance/persona could be effective, how much information should be provided, and what level of specificity would be sufficient. By comparison, the student who is genre savvy and is aware of the various expectations attached to informational writing can choose which genre expectations to guide his or her writing, which to disregard, and if or where to vary the conventional pattern. This genre-savvy student enjoys a tremendous advantage over the first student.

Genre knowledge also supports reading comprehension. If children are familiar with the structure of a text, they can make predictions and understand the functions of text features such as dialogue, and so read more purposefully. Moreover, being familiar with the text structure also makes it easier for readers to internalize the information in a text. Students who understand the organizational pattern of a text can use this knowledge to locate key information, identify what is important and unimportant, synthesize information that appears in different locations within a text, and organize the information in memory. In general, making readers more aware of genre structure appears to improve comprehension, memory, and, thus, learning.

Several genres are fundamental to writing development in kindergarten through fifth grade. The four that are discussed in this book and the others in the grade-by-grade New Standards rubrics series are (1) narrative writing (sharing events, telling stories), (2) report of information (informing others), (3) instructions (instructing others about how to get things done), and (4) responding to literature. The characteristic features of each of these genres are presented in rubrics that describe different levels of performance.

In their current form, the rubrics in this book are not designed to be used with students. They are too complex, and their language is too abstract for children. However, the rubrics can easily serve as templates for guiding the development of grade-level-appropriate classroom rubrics that address elements and strategies. They are, in effect, end-of-the-year targets from which a teacher maps backward to plan instruction.

What Makes a Rubric Good to Use With Students?

Rubrics can be developed and used in formative or summative ways. Typically, rubrics used in summative evaluation are short. They provide a minimum amount of detail so that scorers can quickly and efficiently assign a score to a piece of student writing. Rubrics used in summative assessment are also static, out of necessity. After all, only by using the same rubric can you get comparative data in order to report trends over time. Further, they represent how students are expected to write at the end of a grading period. Summative rubrics don't provide information about the road along the way. Formative rubrics, on the other hand, trace patterns of development and focus on the particular.

Focus on the Particular

The brevity required for efficient scoring and the static nature of summative rubrics fight against what teachers and students need to foster writing development. For example, it is not enough for a writer to be told that his or her writing is "well organized," a phrase commonly found on generic rubrics in state assessments. Such a global statement does not help the writer understand what it takes to make writing well organized. A more effective descriptor would be, "Clearly sequences events in the story and maintains control of point of view."

Be Intelligible

Formative rubrics must also be meaningful to students. Ideally, they should grow out of the work of the classroom and represent a consensus about what constitutes good writing. They must be written in language that the students understand, language that is familiar. The goal is for students to be able to self-assess their writing in order to take on productive revisions and interact with peers in response groups or with the teacher in a conference. The language of the rubric should frame such interactions so that they are meaningful to everyone and grounded in the classroom culture.

Set Targets and Offer Advice

Formative rubrics should set targets and offer advice. At each score level, a good rubric provides a list of criteria that defines performance at that level. Advancement to the next level (the target) comes about by refining the paper to match the criteria in the next score level. So, for example, if a student's paper is at score point 3 and that student wants a score point 4, the student must revise the paper to include all the elements for the higher score currently missing from the paper or must refine the way in which the elements and strategies in his or her paper are developed. Rubrics are not good tools for revision if the distinctions between score levels are set only by qualifiers such as "scant" detail, "some" detail, "adequate" detail, and "effective" detail. Better rubrics provide more definitive distinctions such as "no introduction," "an introduction that names the topic and provides at least minimal context," or "an introduction that names the topic, provides context, and generates reader interest." Better rubrics focus on the features and components of particular genres (for example, in narrative, character development, plot, dialogue, flashback). Such rubrics provide students and teachers with language to talk about the ways certain texts accomplish particular purposes. The rubrics presented in this book encompass both the genre elements and the strategies associated with each genre.

Be Developed in a Classroom Setting

Students and teachers need formative rubrics that emerge from the teaching in a classroom and that specify work yet to be done. To learn about genres, students need to be engaged in active inquiry. Guided by their teachers, they can analyze texts of a published author, a peer, or their own work, and develop classroom rubrics as they examine the texts. The texts will serve as examples and inspiration. These classroom rubrics should be constructed as guidelines to improve student writing performance.

When rubrics are constructed as guidelines to improve performance, it is possible for a student, working alone or with a teacher, to use a rubric as a checklist—a rough approximation of what is in place and how well wrought these elements are. Once that is done, the student should be able to study the criteria at the next level

Report of Information Rubric

	4 Awesome	3 Good	2 So-So	1 Needs Improvement
Organization	A good strong lead that catches the reader's attention.	It has an ok lead. It could be better.	Lead doesn't get the reader's attention.	No lead.
	Middle is completely developed. Facts relate to the controlling idea.	Middle has some interesting facts and details.	Middle has a few facts but not enough info. Facts might not relate to the controlling idea. It may include info. we don't need.	Middle has only opinions and no new information or scattered info. not related to the topic.
	It has closing which ties every thing together.	Thoughtful ending but it does not summarize piece or bring things together.	Ending is weak such as "Bye," "The End" or tries to close but meaning is not clear.	Piece just stops without attempting to close.
Development	The controlling idea is clear. One part connects to the next.	Clearly about one topic but facts, connections and questions are not logically linked.	Topic is there, but the middle is "listy" (like a grocery list) It won't flow logically.	Too many different ideas. The information is not clustered. There is little connection between different info.
Information	Detailed information of "old" and "new" info.	Some explaining of "old" + "new" information	Tries to explain information.	Information is unclear.
Connections	Personal experiences relate to the controlling idea.	Personal experiences are related to the topic. It is not clear how they relate to the controlling idea.	References to personal experiences which are not clear to reader.	Did not make any connections to personal experiences.
Questions	Questions that indicate an inquiry on the part of the writer.	Questions which add to the piece but do not show inquiry.	Questions do not add to the piece.	The piece does not include any questions.
Language	Good word choice. Uses action words. Writer "paints" a picture for the reader. Establishes author as expert.	So so word choice. Words do not come alive. Picture not painted.	Uses everyday words. Not many action or descriptive words.	Language is confusing for the reader.
	No mistakes in mechanics.	Some errors in mechanics which can be easily corrected with a reminder.	Too many mistakes in mechanics that keep this piece from meeting standards. Requires teaching.	Reader is kept from meaning by the mistakes in language and mechanics.

The above is an example of a classroom rubric, constructed jointly by a teacher and her students. This joint construction ensures a shared understanding about what constitutes good writing and about what "next steps" should guide instruction.

to determine what further work would need to be done for the writing to show significant improvement.

In some cases, such as when papers are almost at standard, a simple revision by the student is enough to sufficiently improve the quality of the work. The revision conference would have the teacher providing a reminder, such as, "Did you forget x?" or a suggestion, "Why not flesh out your central character's motivation a bit?" No instruction would be necessary; the writer would just need to be nudged a bit. But in other cases, to bring the paper "up to standard" would require significantly more than a nudge. Many papers signal a substantial need for instruction, time, and practice.

Note: Implicit here are two assumptions. One, that it is the job of the teacher to enable the writer and not just "fix" the paper. And two, that learning to write takes time. In some cases, learning to use the elements that define the next higher score point might take up to a year!

Change With Instruction

Formative rubrics grow. Thoughtful teachers know that they have to move students from their initial performances in September to more refined performances at the end of the year. The instruction they provide will make this change possible. Consider the kindergarten students who begin school with no awareness of the conventions of print. When asked to write a story, they will likely draw a picture and perhaps include some random letters. After instruction, and with time, these students will begin to produce writing that moves from left to right, and top to bottom. They likely will copy words from word charts and play with phonetic spelling. Initial rubrics should celebrate this growth with criteria aimed at moving students forward one step at a time.

Older students, too, will improve with focused instruction and practice. Consider a beginning of the year third-grade classroom in which a teacher is doing a study on narration. The first rubric might have as few as three elements in order to represent what students initially know:

1. Has a beginning that interests the reader
2. Has a number of events that taken together tell a story
3. Has some sort of closure

The three-element rubric captures the essence of narrative and, hence, is complete. A more fully developed narrative rubric would also have some mention of transitions and probably some mention of detail. So, the rubric could easily grow from three to five descriptors, as the teacher provides the necessary instruction.

Growing a Rubric

Changing the Number of Levels

Just as the number of descriptors in a rubric may grow, so may the number of levels. Assume the teacher begins the year with a rubric that has three levels: meets the standard, "great writing"; approaches the standard, "O.K. writing"; and needs more work, "ready for revision." As fewer students produce work that falls below standard, the bottom distinctions can disappear (literally be removed/cut off/marked out). Then what was once work that "meets the standard" can become "approaching a higher standard." This can be determined by teacher and students collaboratively. Similarly, work that "met the standard" can now become "ready for revision." Growing a rubric like this—constantly reexamining how good work must be to earn the highest distinction—is a powerful way to highlight student *growth* in writing.

Changing the Anchor Papers

In themselves, rubrics leave much room for ambiguity. They can be made more explicit by providing examples of what they describe. These examples are called *anchor* papers. When the words on the rubric remain unchanged, but the paper that illustrates the level of performance they describe changes, the rubric is said to be "recalibrated." An example will help here: Assume that the rubric simply states, "Has a beginning that engages the reader." The paper that initially illustrates that concept may have a simple opening sentence/ phrase ("Once upon a time there lived a king" or "On Saturday, I saw light"). If recalibrated, the anchor paper would provide a more complex beginning, for example: a paragraph or longer that sets a plot in motion, an example of dialogue that immediately creates reader interest, a description that is simply riveting (think of the beginning of *Maniac McGee*), or even the resolution of a story told as a flashback.

Understanding These Rubrics

Elements and Strategies

The rubrics in this book are divided into two parts. The first section delineates the elements that are fundamental to the genre, and the second section lays out the strategies writers frequently employ to enhance the genre.

This division of the rubric is intentional. The elements are of critical importance and are foundational to the genre. Until a writer can address the elements with some proficiency, an instructional focus on strategies is misguided. Yet, it is not unusual for instruction to skip from very basic work on introductions and conclusions to an emphasis on lifting the level of language in a piece, most often by inserting metaphors and similes. While figurative language can distinguish a good piece of writing, it cannot compensate for a fundamental lack of development. Think of the compulsories in an Olympic figure skating event. The skater must demonstrate proficiency performing the athletic stunts required by the judges before attempting the more creative dance moves that are also part of his or her repertoire. Genres, likewise, require the writer to address certain elements.

That is not to say that the strategies are unimportant. Frequently, they work with the elements to carry a reader through the text. Consider the work of dialogue in advancing the plot of a novel. The dialogue provides clues about who characters are and what motivates them. Dialogue also frequently helps a reader make transitions when there are scene changes or shifts in time. But a novel without a well-developed plot, well-developed characters, or some organizational frame will not be made whole simply with the inclusion of dialogue.

Too often, writing instruction in narrative focuses on leads and transitions to structure chronological ordering and on teaching strategies out of context (for instance, including dialogue for the sake of having dialogue, rather than as a strategy to develop character or advance the action). In many classrooms, not enough time is spent on the elements, the "compulsories" of genres. For this reason, the rubrics have been designed to emphasize both strategies and elements. When teachers use the rubrics to analyze students' strengths and weaknesses in order to plan instruction, they should first focus on the elements section. The strategies can be folded in instructionally as students begin to demonstrate awareness of the elements. In some cases, young writers will likely pick up strategies on their own through their reading and by appropriating text from favorite authors.

Note: The lists of elements and strategies provided in these materials are foundational. They are not meant to be exhaustive or exclusive.

Except at the kindergarten level, the scores for the New Standards rubrics are distributed across five levels:

- Score point 5: Work that exceeds the grade-level standard
- Score point 4: Work that meets the standard
- Score point 3: Work that needs only a conference
- Score point 2: Work that needs instruction
- Score point 1: Work that needs substantial support

Score Point 5

Papers at this score point go well beyond grade-level expectations. What sets score point 5 papers apart is the level of sophistication brought to the text by the writer. Occasionally, this sophistication is reflected in the writer's syntax or vocabulary. Sometimes the sophistication is shown by a nuanced execution of writing strategies. Other times it may simply be the level of development that comes from the writer's deep understanding of the topic or the genre. In all cases, what distinguishes a score point 5 is writing development that goes beyond what the school curriculum has provided that writer. Performance at this level is exceptional, beyond what might be expected even after a year's program of effective instruction. This is not to say that students writing at score point 5 could not benefit from instruction. Even adult professional writers work to hone their craft. There are many strategies that a writer can learn and work to refine, and these should be the basis for the teacher's instructional plan for exceptional writers.

Score Point 4

Papers at this score point illustrate a standards-setting performance. They are a full representation of the genre, though some features may be better executed than others.

Score point 4 papers grow out of good teaching, student effort, and quite likely a genre-specific curriculum. These papers "meet the standard" for what students should be able to accomplish if they receive effective instruction.

Note: The criteria that define score points 5 and 4 are identical. This is intentional. What distinguishes a 5 from a 4 is not the presence or absence of a particular element or strategy. Rather, it is the overall quality of execution and the level of language the writer employs. The writers of score point 5 papers frequently also bring something to the text that may not be provided by instruction—a deep understanding or passion for the topic and the genre.

Score Point 3

Generally, the papers at score point 3 do not meet the standard for one of two reasons: (1) the writer did not include a necessary feature, such as a conclusion, or (2) the execution of a strategy was not well done. In either case, the writer of a paper at score point 3 is otherwise competent and needs only a conference to point out the paper's problem in order to revise it upward to a score point 4. The suggestions for improving the paper should come from the criteria at score point 4.

Score point 3 papers are not unusual with novice writers. Many young writers, for example, produce reports without an introduction because they assume that the title of their piece is sufficient to introduce the topic. Or they may not accommodate their readers by providing sufficient detail or a satisfactory ending. Such writers are completely capable of improving these inadequacies when they are pointed out in a teacher–student conference. It is these papers that represent score point 3. To achieve the target of score point 4, a teacher needs only to point out omissions from the criteria listed at score point 4 or the need for refinement in a revision.

Score Point 2

The student writer of a score point 2 paper needs instruction in order to produce work that is up to standard. A quick read-through of the score point 2 paper makes obvious either that there are gaps in the writer's understanding of the genre features or that the writer simply has insufficient control over the strategy he or she is attempting. The instructional next steps are suggested by criteria at score point 4. However, it is almost certain that student work will pass through some of the inadequacies suggested by score point 3 before the writer can produce work that meets standard. The student producing writing at score point 2 needs instruction and practice with feedback. Deep understanding and resulting proficiency could take several months.

Score Point 1

Papers that receive a score point 1 are representative of a writer who needs substantial support. The student writer at score point 1 may need extensive help developing basic fluency and basic genre knowledge to move toward meeting the standard. The criteria at score point 4 outline a map for the student's development. To move from habitually producing work at a score point 1 to typically producing work at a score point 4 will require much support and time, perhaps as much as a year. Along with the classroom support from the teacher, students who write papers at score point 1 may require access to other kinds of safety nets, such as special programs, in order to make progress toward meeting the standard.

How to Use These Rubrics

Research, as well as practical experience, demonstrate that within any single classroom the range of performance in writing and in children's knowledge of genres is wide. In any particular grade, some students' papers will look like the work of children in earlier grades, whereas the work of other students will appear more advanced. Even the work of a single child will show great variation from day to day because development does not progress smoothly forward in step-by-step increments. Moreover, skills that appear to be mastered are sometimes thrown into disarray as new skills are acquired.

We also know that students write some genres better than others. Research shows that young children typically have more experience with narrative genres than scientific or poetic genres. Research also shows that children are more successful handling the familiar structure of stories than the less familiar structure of arguments. One explanation for these differences may lie in the instruction about genres children receive, or do not receive, in school. Another explanation may be related to their experiences outside of school. If children have had infrequent exposure to particular genres, they will be less adept at writing and reading them than children who have had frequent exposure.

To use these rubrics, a teacher should first ask each student to produce a piece of writing specific to a particular genre. If the genre is narrative, the teacher might say, "I'd like you to write a story about…." If the genre is informational, the teacher might say, "I'd like you to write a report about…." If the genre is instructional writing, "I'd like you to write a paper explaining how to do something." Or if the genre is response to literature, "I'd like you to read this story/book/poem and then write a paper that explains what the author is saying." A response to literature by kindergarten students might be phrased as, "I'd like you to listen as I read and then write a response."

Once the student writing is in hand, the teacher should analyze individual performances with the appropriate genre rubric. This analysis will indicate what kinds of instruction are needed for students to gain the knowledge and skills required to produce work in that genre at score point 4 (meets the standard).

Note: Making a judgment about proficiency on the basis of a single sample is always chancy. To have a better sense of a student's proficiency, it is always wise to look at several samples.

It is almost certain that student work will not reflect the same level of proficiency for each element or strategy contained in the rubric. That is, a student writer may establish a strong orientation and context (score point 4), but develop character only weakly (score point 2). The student could make good use of dialogue (score point 4), but provide too few details (score point 2). In fact, most papers produced by novice writers are of this uneven quality.

The point of these rubrics is not to assign an overall score to student work, as one might do in a formal assessment, and certainly not to assign a grade. Rather, it is to highlight for teachers the characteristics of student work at different levels of performance so that appropriate instruction and feedback can be provided. Grading student writing is a necessity for teachers, and it is essential that the grades assigned reflect student performance relative to the genre elements and strategies. Grades can be derived from the classroom rubric. See the sample classroom rubric on page 3.

How to Use the Papers and Commentary

Papers at each score point are representative of what work at that score level might look like. They are concrete examples of what the rubric describes. The commentaries describe the student writing in relation to the rubric. Teachers can use the papers and commentaries to calibrate the levels of performance of their own students. Comparing their students' work with the work in this book will highlight for teachers the various levels of proficiency among their students and facilitate instructional planning. Students in upper-elementary grades can study the papers as models of work that represent either a strong performance for a genre, or work that could be strengthened through revision. Teachers can use the commentaries to scaffold discussion, and working together, teachers and students can construct classroom rubrics. A further use for the papers and commentaries is as the focus for teacher meetings where the goal is to establish a shared understanding of what good writing looks like.

In all cases, the commentaries have been written with the intention of honoring what is in place in the papers. Too often, student assessment focuses entirely on what is missing and what is poorly done. This genre-based approach to writing assumes that writing development is a layered process in which new learning builds over time upon what is already in place. The starting point is always first to identify the paper's strengths. In this manner, writing assessment is a positive, additive process, one that is also transparent and meaningful to students.

At the end of each of the commentaries for papers at score points 3, 2, and 1, there is a set of "next-step" suggestions. For score point 3 papers, the set is titled Possible Conference Topics; at score point 2, Next Steps in Instruction; and at score point 1, Roadmap for Development. These different titles are indicative of the kind and amount of support a student will need to produce work that meets the standard (for instance, a short conference at score point 3 versus extended instruction at score point 2). All of these next-step suggestions are simply that—suggestions. It may well be that other sets of suggestions could also work. However, the suggestions provided were drawn from an analysis of dozens of papers typical of that score point, as well as from an analysis of the particular paper described in the commentary. These suggestions were also derived from the rubric criteria at score point 4.

It should be emphasized that students at score point 2 and score point 1 will not move from these score levels without passing through the next higher score level(s). Writing proficiency takes time and practice. There will be some slow steps forward and some backsliding on the students' part. But these are novice writers, so patience, practice, and coaching should be part of any instructional plan.

This book has been designed with insight into the complexities of teaching writing. It includes student work as models and lists of rubric criteria as scales, two things that, according to George Hillocks (1984), research indicates will improve student writing if used appropriately. This book was drawn from the work of dedicated teachers and hard-working students. (To protect their privacy, names have been removed.) Admittedly, this is only one part of a comprehensive writing program, but it will serve well those teachers who use it to plan for student instruction.

The student papers in this book were chosen from more than 5,000 pieces written by students in many different elementary schools in several different school districts. The papers illustrate the range of abilities and performance of students at different grade levels from kindergarten through fifth grade, as well as ranges within grade levels. In the first year of the project, 3,586 students participated. Their teachers taught author and genre studies, and at the end of the year, the teachers collected portfolios of student writing. The examples in this book are drawn from these students' portfolios.

Narrative

Narrative is the genre most commonly associated with elementary schools. In fact, people assume that narrative, or more specifically, story, is the purview of our youngest students. To a large extent this assumption is logical. Elementary school is filled with story—picture books, show and tell, dramas, and basal readers. Children make sense of their lives and their worlds through story. Jerome Bruner (1985) tells us, "They [young children] are not able to...organize things in terms of cause and effect and relationships, so they turn things into stories, and when they try to make sense of their life they use the storied version of their experience as the basis for further reflection. If they don't catch something in a narrative structure, it doesn't get remembered very well, and it doesn't seem to be accessible for further kinds of mulling over."

Narratives have time as their deep structure. A narrative involves a series of events that can be plotted out on some sort of time line. The time span could be short, a few moments, or long, even across generations.

There are many kinds of narratives (frequently called subgenres): memoirs, biographies, accounts, anecdotes, folktales, recounts, mysteries, autobiographies, etc. Recount is a kind of narrative in which the teller simply retells events for the purpose of informing or entertaining. Anecdotes, on the other hand, generally include some kind of crisis that generates an emotional reaction—frustration, satisfaction, insecurity, etc. Stories, in contrast, exhibit a somewhat different pattern. A complication creates a problem, which then has to be overcome (the resolution). Stories are built of events that are causally linked (the events recounted share a cause–effect relationship). Think for a moment about stories. It is quite easy to say of them, "this happened because this happened, so this happened and that caused this to happen." Narrative accounts, by contrast, are comprised of a series of events that in total may or may not add up to anything significant other than the reader's sense of "this is how things went." It is a matter of "this happened and then this and then this and then this." Folktales take yet another form. Like other genres, different subgenres of narrative can serve different purposes, for example, to entertain or to make a point about what people should do, or about how the world should be.

The New Standards expectation for student writers around narrative requires that they be able to craft a narrative account, either fiction or nonfiction, that does the following: establishes a context; creates a point of view; establishes a situation or plot; creates an organizing structure; provides detail to develop the event sequence and characters; uses a range of appropriate strategies, such as dialogue; and provides closure.

Orientation and Context

As it relates to narrative, orienting the reader and providing context usually involves bringing readers into the narrative (situating them somehow in the story line) and engaging them.

There are many ways to do this, of course, but among the most common strategies are

- Introducing a character who is somehow interesting
- Establishing a situation that intrigues or startles a reader
- Situating a reader in a time or place
- Having a narrator speak directly to the reader in order to create empathy or interest

From this initial grounding, writers can begin to develop the event sequence of their narratives.

Plot Development and Organization

The organization of narrative is not necessarily a straightforward chronological ordering of events. Consider just a few variations. Narratives frequently are organized as the simultaneously ongoing, unfolding of events in the lives of multiple persons or fictional characters. The end of such a narrative requires that several or all of these persons' or characters' lives come together. In some narratives, the sequence of events may be altered to create interest, so the writer may use flashbacks and flash-forwards to move the characters around in time or to create a "backstory" of the events leading up to the story. Stories within a story are another commonly used device. Mystery stories often are organized by laying out an initiating event (crime), and then providing a series of clues and several false resolutions before the truth is finally revealed. Newspaper stories traditionally flow from the standard "who, what, where, when, why, how?" of an introductory paragraph. Memoir is organized around a single event or series of events that sum up the essence of who someone is, or was, and what values and heritage shaped that person. Biography and autobiography usually begin with birth and move through early years, adolescent years, and late years of someone's life. The diversity of narrative genres, as well as the myriad ways in which they can be developed, serve to remind us of the various options writers have for communicating with readers.

In general, however, narratives are often organized in such a way that some event precipitates a causally linked series of further events, which in some way is ultimately resolved. Episodes share a relationship to each other and usually are built around a problem and emotional response, an action, and an outcome. Nuanced plotting frequently involves subplots, built through episodes, and shifts in time. The classic plot structures for conflict are man vs. man, man vs. society, man vs. nature, and man vs. self.

Although children and adults may tell complicated narratives, it is important to remember that they also tell simple recounts. Recounts tell what happened, and organization is based on a series of events that all relate to a particular occasion. Children often recount personal narratives about school excursions or particularly memorable events in their lives—their immigration to America, the death of a cherished pet, the birth of a sister, and so on. In recounts, sometimes there is not an initiating event; rather, writers present a bed-to-bed story that retells the mundane events of the day.

Adult writers use a variety of methods to develop event sequences and their settings. They typically develop settings by providing details about place, colors, structures, landscape, and so on. They use several techniques to manage event sequences and time, including flashbacks and flash-forwards, forecasting, and back stories. They sometimes manipulate time by compressing or expanding it, that is, by providing pacing. They use dialogue and interior monologue purposefully to advance the action. During the elementary school years, children are just beginning to master these techniques.

Because narratives are based on events in time, writers also often use linking words that deal with time and the organization of events (then, before, after, when, while). When people recount events, they often refer to the specific times when events happened (yesterday, last summer). As children mature, their repertoire of temporal signals develops, from simple transition words (then, after, before) to more complex phrases ("At the time...") and clauses ("Before he went in the house...").

Character/Narrator Development

Adult writers use a variety of techniques to develop characters, and in some cases, the persona of the narrator. They describe their physical characteristics, their personalities, their actions and gestures, their emotional reactions to events, and through dialogue and internal monologue, their internal motivations and goals. Whether narratives include real people or fictional characters, the personalities, motivations, and reactions of the narrator and the characters are often central to the development of the narrative. When children develop characters, some are "stock characters" that regularly inhabit children's stories, such as the mean teacher, the school bully, and the wicked witch. Other characters are more fully and uniquely developed through description, dialogue, and other narrative techniques.

Although children may produce narratives in which fictional characters are fairly well developed, they are less likely to develop the persona of the narrator. And, when they are producing simple recounts of events in their lives, neither the people in their narrative nor the persona of the narrator may be particularly well developed. In simple recounts, the focus is more likely to be on what people did than on their motives or reactions.

Closure

Writers bring closure to narratives in a variety of ways. Structurally, they achieve closure by providing a resolution to a problem (or a failed resolution). But they also provide closure with a variety of overt signals—with evaluations that inform the reader what the narrator thought about the events, with comments that serve to tie up loose ends in the narrative or bridge the gap between the narrative and the present, and with typical ending markers such as "the end" and "they all lived happily ever after." As children mature, their strategies for providing closure become more sophisticated and their repertoire of strategies more broad.

Narrative in Fifth Grade

When writing narratives, some students at fifth grade will still be struggling to develop reader interest when they introduce their narratives. They typically establish a context, but they may begin their stories in routine ways ("I went to the delta over the summer vacation. But there is one memory that sticks out the most."). They may create the kind of "bed-to-bed" narrative in which incidents are related with more or less equal weight, showing little or no selectivity in the events they portray. They may attempt pacing, but be unable to carry it off. Their characters may be undeveloped, and they may make little or no use of dialogue in character development. They typically provide closure, but they may have few strategies for doing so. They may employ simple closing statements ("I had lots of fun at the delta but the bat experience just scares me.") or formal markers ("The end.").

Students who meet the standard orient and engage the reader, set the time, identify the place, and introduce characters, or they begin in the middle of the action to catch the reader's interest, and then backfill the orienting information ("The car pulled in the driveway like a topper dropping sail. Just kidding. Jack and George, both of them short, blond and freckly, hopped out of the car and ran around the yard as if they'd been burned."). They purposefully select and order occurrences to create a series of elaborated events that unfold naturally. They employ a variety of temporal words, phrases, and clauses ("A little while later..."; "After the shock..."; "This year's prank..."; "In the summer..."), and they use verb tense, temporal words, and literary language to shift with relative ease from one time frame to another ("Saoirse and Morraha had been planning this journey for exactly one year and a day..."; "It was now morning..."). Fifth graders who meet the standard are also selective about the information they present, and they shift with relative ease between narrative sequencing and description. They employ a variety of techniques to provide closure to their writing, such as the circle story format; a short, telling sentence; a reflection; or a surprise ending.

Students who meet the standard at fifth grade are able to create complex characters. They provide insights about the characters or the persona of the narrator by describing internal thoughts, feelings, or desires ("I was paralyzed with fear."; "My heart suddenly felt proud of myself."; "There is something immensely satisfying about having people flinch when you walk by...") as well as external reactions ("Jake's face was now as white and pale as a ghost."). In addition, their syntax and vocabulary are often more complex than the vocabulary and syntax of writers who do not meet the standard. Their sentence structure and vocabulary reflect a developing proficiency with written text and a deepening understanding of language. In sum, at fifth grade, students who meet the standard typically have a wide repertoire of narrative options and flexibility in using them.

Narrative Rubrics Elements

	5 Exceeds Standard*	4 Meets Standard
Orientation and Context	• Orients and engages the reader (e.g., sets the time, indicates the location where the story takes place, introduces character(s), or enters immediately into the story line).	• Orients and engages the reader (e.g., sets the time, indicates the location where the story takes place, introduces character(s), or enters immediately into the story line).
Plot Development and Organization	• Creates a series of events or incidents. • Organizes the text; purposefully selects and orders events. • Paces the narrative to highlight the significance of events or incidents, to create drama or suspense, etc. • Elaborates key events, incidents, and actions, including a focal event. • Omits irrelevant incidents or events.	• Creates a series of events or incidents. • Organizes the text; purposefully selects and orders events. • Paces the narrative to highlight the significance of events or incidents, to create drama or suspense, etc. • Elaborates key events, incidents, and actions, including a focal event. • Omits irrelevant incidents or events.
Character/ Narrator Development	• Develops complex characters or provides insights about the persona of the narrator (e.g., by describing the character's or narrator's actions or internal thoughts, feelings, desires, fears).	• Develops complex characters or provides insights about the persona of the narrator (e.g., by describing the character's or narrator's actions or internal thoughts, feelings, desires, fears).
Closure	• Provides closure with one or more strategies (e.g., a circle story format, a reflection, a surprise ending).	• Provides closure with one or more strategies (e.g., a circle story format, a reflection, a surprise ending).

	3 Needs Revision	2 Needs Instruction	1 Needs Substantial Support
Orientation and Context	• Orients and engages the reader (e.g., sets the time, indicates the location where the story takes place, introduces the character(s), or enters immediately into the story line).	• Establishes a context (e.g., time, place, or occasion). • May attempt to develop reader interest.	• Establishes a context (e.g., time, place, or occasion). • Typically does not develop reader interest.
Plot Development and Organization	• Creates a series of incidents or events. • Provides some pacing.	• Creates a series of incidents or events. • May not be selective in describing events. • Attempts to provide pacing.	• Creates a series of incidents or events; typically is not selective in describing events. • Provides a simple recounting of events or incidents with no pacing.
Character/ Narrator Development	• Includes some character development (e.g., by describing the character's or narrator's actions or internal thoughts, feelings, desires, fears).	• Includes minimal character development.	• Includes little or no character development.
Closure	• Provides closure with one or more strategies (e.g., a circle story format, a reflection, a surprise ending).	• May use simple concluding statements or formal markers (e.g., "The End").	• May use simple concluding statements or formal markers (e.g., "The End").

*The criteria that define score points 5 and 4 are identical. This is intentional. What distinguishes a 5 from a 4 is not the presence or absence of a particular element or strategy. Rather, it is the overall quality of execution and the level of language the writer employs. Writers of score point 5 papers bring something to the text that may not be provided by instruction—a deep understanding or passion for the topic and the genre.

Narrative Rubrics Strategies

	5 Exceeds Standard*	4 Meets Standard
Detail	• Uses details selectively (e.g., to describe action, create images, develop characters or persona of the narrator).	• Uses details selectively (e.g., to describe action, create images, develop characters or persona of the narrator).
Dialogue	• Dialogue, if present, is used purposefully (e.g., to advance the action, to develop characters, or to provide background information for the reader).	• Dialogue, if present, is used purposefully (e.g., to advance the action, to develop characters, or to provide background information for the reader).
Other	• Uses literary language (e.g., "quick as lightning she ran away"). • Uses temporal words, phrases, and clauses to indicate shifts in time (e.g., "After a long while…").	• Uses literary language (e.g., "quick as lightning she ran away"). • Uses temporal words, phrases, and clauses to indicate shifts in time (e.g., "After a long while…").

	3 Needs Revision	2 Needs Instruction	1 Needs Substantial Support
Detail	• Includes details, but may not use them selectively.	• Provides few details.	• Provides few details.
Dialogue	• Dialogue, if present, may not be used purposefully (e.g., to advance the action, to develop characters, or to provide background information for the reader).	• Dialogue, if present, may not be used purposefully (e.g., to advance the action, to develop characters, or to provide background information for the reader).	• Dialogue, if present, typically is not used purposefully (e.g., to advance the action, to develop characters, or to provide background information for the reader).
Other	• May use literary language. • Uses temporal words, phrases, and clauses to indicate shifts in time.	• May use literary language. • Uses temporal words, phrases, and clauses.	• May use literary language. • Uses temporal words, phrases, and clauses.

*The criteria that define score points 5 and 4 are identical. This is intentional. What distinguishes a 5 from a 4 is not the presence or absence of a particular element or strategy. Rather, it is the overall quality of execution and the level of language the writer employs. Writers of score point 5 papers bring something to the text that may not be provided by instruction—a deep understanding or passion for the topic and the genre.

Score Point 5

Narrative Student Work and Commentary: "Saoirse"

Chapter 1

Saoirse

"I will someday sail around the world seeking new lands and treasure", Saoirse said boldly to her older sister, Columbine.

"Oh, will you? I don't see how you could ever want to be on a frightening ship knowing you could die at sea. I ask you why, my sister would you seek such a dangerous life? And then who would marry you?" Columbine asked as she lovingly brushed her hair with a jewelled comb.

"For adventure Columbine! Don't you see how exciting it would be? And anyway I don't plan on getting married", Saoirse answered.

Saoirse was twelve and Columbine seventeen. They lived in a castle near the River Lee in the Medieval, Irish town of Cork.

Saoirse could no longer stand the constant nagging from her parents about how naughty

-1-

This carefully controlled piece describes Saoirse's quest to discover the source of her magic pouch, and the story details the adventures of Saoirse and her friend Morraha. The writer successfully incorporates many of the conventions of quest narratives found in texts such as *Harry Potter* and the *Lord of the Rings* trilogy, including subplots, long-lost relatives, and search for treasure. "Saoirse" exceeds the standard for narrative writing at fifth grade. We present selected pages here to illustrate the elements and strategies of student writers.

The author orients and engages the reader in the first chapter by beginning with dialogue that characterizes the main character and foreshadows the events of the story ("'I will someday sail around the world seeking new lands and treasure,' Saoirse said boldly."). The writer orients the reader by providing key details about the story's setting ("the Medieval, Irish town of Cork") and the characters (Saoirse is a rebellious girl who craves adventure and does not fit in with the rest of her family).

The narrative unfolds in a series of events that details the adventures of Saoirse and Morraha. The narrative is ordered purposefully (they both run away to find out more about themselves, and they soon meet Pooka, who knows Saoirse's real family and who is Morraha's grandfather). The text elaborates on key events (such as Saoirse and Morraha's introduction to Pooka), but omits irrelevant detail.

The author uses chapter breaks to pace the narrative; they highlight the significance of events and create suspense. For instance, Saoirse and Morraha

Score Point 5 *continued*

she was and why couldn't she be proper - like her sister. She was running away. "I just don't fit in," Saoirse said to herself.

Packing her things into her red woven sack she reviewed the long journey ahead of her. She would meet her friend Morraha at the willow tree by the shipping wharf. There was one large ship anchored amongst the smaller ones. Together they would sneak on board and hide in the captain's quarters.

Saoirse and Morraha had been planning this journey for exactly one year and a day, gathering supplies and figuring out how to escape.

Saoirse packed her maps, books, food, clothes, and her magic fairy dust to protect her against all evil. Inside was this spell:

"Fairies dancing in the sky
Come and help me,
help me fly."

She didn't know were she got it or who gave it to her, nor did her parents. But on this journey she, Saoirse, would find out who or what gave her this pouch.

"All right, I can't wait forever, I better go," Saoirse thought to herself. She packed one last thing into her sack, her sword which had a dragon's

-@-2-@-

hide in the apple bins on the ship, and the chapter ends by foreshadowing the importance of the hiding place ("They also didn't realize that these barrels would soon change their lives forever.").

The writer develops complex characters through the use of dialogue and detail (for instance, Saoirse's sword has a dragon on its hilt; Saoirse feels safe with Pooka because his voice is "dragon-like"; Saoirse discovers that she has a gift for talking to dragons).

The writer provides a satisfying sense of closure to the story by tying up Saoirse's story (she finds her "real family"), as well as those of Morraha (he returns to live with his mother and Pooka) and Saoirse's "fake sister" Princess Columbine (she marries the insensitive Captain Snuff). The ending also leaves the door open for a sequel.

This piece includes selective details that develop the character (the glossary tells readers Saoirse means "'Freedom' in ancient Irish language," and the meaning of her name provides further insight into her character).

The dialogue advances the action and develops characters. For instance, when Morraha tries to defend Saoirse from Pooka, Saoirse says, "Oh and by the way, I can defend myself, Morraha." The sentence reminds readers that Saoirse is fiercely independent.

The piece includes literary language such as that found in quest stories ("Then as quick as lightning she ran away toward the port. Towards freedom!").

The piece includes temporal words, phrases, and clauses to indicate shifts in time ("With that..."; "Once inside..."; "It was now morning...").

Score Point 5 *continued*

head on the hilt, its tail wrapped around the blade.

With that she snuck out the window and climbed down the vines to the ground. Then as quick as lightning she ran away toward the port. Towards freedom!

Chapter 2
-⊙- Among the Apples -⊙-

Saoirse was the first one there. A little while later Morraha came running to the tree.

"What took you so long?" Saoirse asked him.

"I had to wait 'til Mammy went to sleep," Morraha answered when he had caught his breath.

"O.K," said Saoirse with a shrug, "Let's go!"

Running quietly toward the ship they each hoped they wouldn't be caught and sent home.

"The cost is clear," Morraha whispered to her.

-⊙-3-⊙-

They jumped up in the boat, which was empty and ran toward the captains quarters. Once inside they took hiding in two barrels. They didn't realize that the old oaken barrels contained apples for the voyage. They also didn't realize that these barrels would soon change their lives forever.

Chapter 3
-⊙- Three Voices -⊙-

It was now morning and the sailers were boarding the boat. Saoirse and Morraha had just woken up and were eating some apples. Suddenly they heard foot steps coming into the captain's room! They held their breath and stayed quiet. Then another pair of foot steps came in. Then voices- a grumpy voice who sounded like he was very conceited and a voice so wise and old - it remined Saoirse of a dragon who had lived a long time and seen it all.

"I want all of the sailers on board by sunrise or they

-⊙-4-⊙-

Score Point 5 continued

will be left behind," said the grumpy voice.
"Yes sir, right away sir," said a different voice they had not heard before. It was a high-pitched voice and Saoirse guessed him to be the cabin boy.
Then the wise-dragon-voice spoke, taking out his load stone, "My load stone tells me North is the way Captain, the way to the Dragon Island and all the worlds beyond. The journey shall be a long one, Captain."
Saoirse liked the dragon-like voice already.

Chapter 4
The Journey Begins

"All rise and greet the master, Captain Snuff," shouted the cabin boy when the crew was gathered on deck. Claps rose up from every one.
Captain Snuff bowed and said pompously, "Now I would like to introduce to you our navigator, Pooka."
Pooka rose and his dragon-voice said these words-

-5-

"By the name of our guides Fire, Earth, Water, and Sky let this trip to the Dragon Island and the worlds beyond begin!"
They lifted the anchor and sailed into the deep magical sea. Then Pooka went below into the captain's quarters to get an apple.

Chapter 5
Princess of the Fairies

Pooka reached into a barrel and withdrew an apple core. e peeked his head inside, curious to know what had eaten he apples. He expected to see rats but instead he spied the top of Saoirse's dark-haired head with apple cores all around her.
"What are you doing here? Are you a stow-away?" Pooka exclaimed, "I could get fired! Captain Snuff might think I brought you on board!"

-6-

Score Point 5 *continued*

"Leave her alone, you big ugly hermit!" said Morraha blasting open the barrel he was in.

Pooka laughed, "I'm sorry lad, I thought you were rats!"

"We're sorry too. We thought you might throw us overboard," Saoirse answered, "oh and by the way, I can defend myself, Morraha."

Morraha answered, "I'm sorry too sir. I didn't know you would be nice like this. I guess I over-reacted a little," Morraha said. "You won't tell anyone will you?"

"No, of course not, would you mind telling me your names again and why you're here?" Pooka answered. He looked first at Saoirse then at Morraha.

"I'm Saoirse and I'm running away from home because I dont really belong. I mean with my parents, Queen Brigid and King Brian and my sister, Princess Columbine. I'm going to find out who or what gave me this pouch," she continued as she took it out to show him. "It's magic fairy dust to protect me against all evil." Then she read the spell,

"Fairies dancing in the sky
come and help me,
help me fly."

"I don't know what it means; I'm trying to find out," Saoirse said sadly.

Pooka's eyes were twinkling like the sea on a summer's day. Suddenly his eyes changed, excited eyes boiling with

-7-

thought, "But I think I do!"

"How?" Saoirse asked excitedly.

"Saoirse is your name, correct?" Pooka asked.

"Correct," Saoirse answered.

"Well Saoirse is a fairy name, a fairy princess name actually. I know this because on one of my voyages I came across a fairy village and the king and Queen of the fairies were looking for their long lost daughter, Princess Saoirse! It must be you!" Pooka said, amazed.

Saoirse said nothing at first, then it all came together. It all made sense - the pouch, the spell, the fairies, her fake family, and herself, Saoirse, Princess of the fairies!

-8-

Assessment Summary: "Saoirse"

ELEMENTS		
	Exceeds Standard	**Commentary**
Orientation and Context	• Orients and engages the reader (e.g., sets the time, indicates the location where the story takes place, introduces character(s), or enters immediately into the story line).	The author orients and engages the reader in chapter one by beginning with dialogue that characterizes the main character and foreshadows the events of the story ("'I will someday sail around the world seeking new lands and treasure,' Saoirse said boldly."). The writer orients the reader by providing key details about the story's setting ("the Medieval, Irish town of Cork") and the characters (Saoirse is a rebellious girl who craves adventure and does not fit in with the rest of her family).
Plot Development and Organization	• Creates a series of events or incidents. • Organizes the text; purposefully selects and orders events. • Paces the narrative to highlight the significance of events or incidents, to create drama or suspense, etc. • Elaborates key events, incidents, and actions, including a focal event. • Omits irrelevant incidents, or events.	The narrative unfolds in a series of events that details the adventures of Saoirse and Morraha. The narrative is ordered purposefully (they both run away to find out more about themselves, and they soon meet Pooka, who knows Saoirse's real family and who is Morraha's grandfather). The author uses chapter breaks to pace the narrative; they highlight the significance of events and create suspense. For instance, Saoirse and Morraha hide in the apple bins on the ship, and the chapter ends by foreshadowing the importance of the hiding place ("They also didn't realize that these barrels would soon change their lives forever."). The text elaborates on key events (such as Saoirse and Morraha's introduction to Pooka), but omits irrelevant detail.
Character/Narrator Development	• Develops complex characters or provides insights about the persona of the narrator (e.g., by describing the character's or narrator's actions or internal thoughts, feelings, desires, fears).	The writer develops complex characters through the use of dialogue and detail (for instance, Saoirse's sword has a dragon on its hilt; Saoirse feels safe with Pooka because his voice is "dragon-like"; Saoirse discovers that she has a gift for talking to dragons).
Closure	• Provides closure with one or more strategies (e.g., a circle story format, a reflection, a surprise ending).	The writer provides a satisfying sense of closure to the story by tying up Saoirse's story (she finds her "real family"), as well as those of Morraha (he returns to live with his mother and Pooka) and Saoirse's "fake sister" Princess Columbine (she marries the insensitive Captain Snuff). The ending also leaves the door open for a sequel.

STRATEGIES		
	Exceeds Standard	**Commentary**
Detail	• Uses details selectively (e.g., to describe action, create images, develop characters or persona of the narrator).	This piece includes selective details that develop character (the glossary tells readers Saoirse means "'Freedom' in ancient Irish language," and the meaning of her name provides further insight into her character).
Dialogue	• Dialogue, if present, is used purposefully (e.g., to advance the action, to develop characters, or to provide background information for the reader).	The dialogue advances the action and develops characters. For instance, when Morraha tries to defend Saoirse from Pooka, Saoirse says, "Oh and by the way, I can defend myself, Morraha." The sentence reminds readers that Saoirse is fiercely independent.
Other	• Uses literary language (e.g., "quick as lightning she ran away"). • Uses temporal words, phrases, and clauses to indicate shifts in time (e.g., "After a long while...").	The piece includes literary language such as that found in quest stories ("Then as quick as lightning she ran away toward the port. Towards freedom!"). The piece includes temporal words, phrases, and clauses to indicate shifts in time ("With that..."; "Once inside..."; "It was now morning...").
Note: The commentary highlights the elements and strategies in the student paper, focusing on how well the paper addresses the totality of the elements and strategies rather than on whether each is included.		

Score Point 4

Narrative Student Work and Commentary: "Getting Shot and Living Through It"

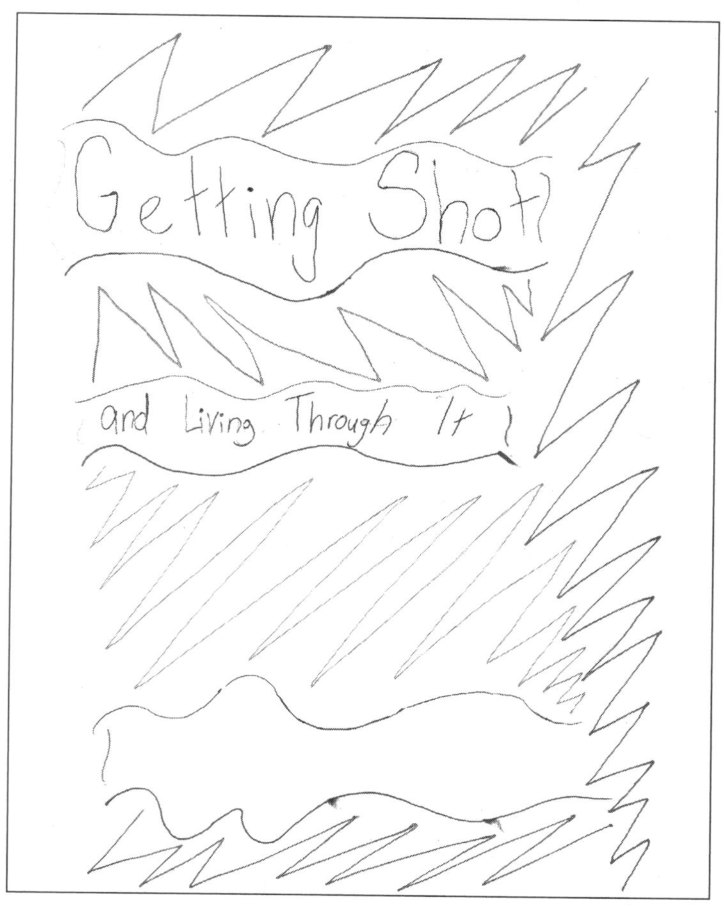

"Getting Shot and Living Through It" is an example of a paper that meets the standard for fifth-grade narrative writing. The author describes his experience getting a malaria shot, and he engages readers by building tension as he details how his anxiety grows while he waits for the shot.

The writer orients and engages the reader by setting the scene in the opening paragraph (he and his family are sitting in the "darkness filled, mountain-top cold, waiting room" and "preparing for the shots of our lives").

The story includes a series of events that are ordered purposefully (he and his family sit in the waiting room in fear; the nurse calls them back into an examining room; he sees his little brother get a shot; he gets a shot).

The writer paces the narrative to create suspense by describing his dread in the waiting room and the fear he feels while he watches his brother get the first shot.

The writer develops the persona of the first-person narrator by including information about his experiences ("I had had shots before. They were not your best friend.") and internal thoughts ("It was like knowing you would be put to sleep, sent to

We were in the darkness filled, mountain-top cold, waiting room. We were preparing for the shots of our lives. Getting shots for malaria and more.

There were many benches all shoved to the right. It was hard to see the color in the murky dark but it seemed to be some sort of faded brown. The room was big, no, huge which gave it all the more reason to be terror bringing. Who knew what would be lurking in the corner! Rats, monsters, anything! There were also doors. Three doors, which were also brown and also faded. One was the way in. Not the way out unfortunately. Another was the way to the other evil places. With the evil hallway and the evil office. The last door was the most evil, The Shot Room.

The rest of the room was filled with families. Including my family of five. My five year old self,

the dementors, waiting to take a ride in the Electric Chair."). He elaborates on key moments, such as his fear in the waiting room, but omits irrelevant information.

The writer provides a sense of closure by describing the sunlight outside the dark, cold doctor's office and by describing his relief ("It was over. All over. Finally.").

The details about the waiting room create an image of the scene ("The room was big, no, huge which gave it all the more reason to be terror bringing.").

The dialogue advances the action (the nurse calling their names), and the interior monologue helps readers understand the narrator's fear.

The writer uses literary language in this piece ("dementor," a word from *Harry Potter*).

The writer manipulates sentence structures for effect ("Who knew what would be lurking in the corner! Rats, monsters, anything!").

The piece includes temporal words, phrases, and clauses ("Before the shot..."; "When Taryn had her turn..."; "But then I remembered...").

Score Point 4 continued

my three year old brother, and my one year old sister. Then there was my mom and dad. Some of the other children were screeching or crying or not knowing what would happen to them. So they would just be playing. I was in the midde of both. I was playing with fear, playing, knowing what would happen, knowing that the worst moment of my life was coming ever closer. It was like knowing you would be put to sleep, sent to the dementors, waiting to take a ride in the Electric Chair.

I had had shots before. They were not your best friend. After a long while a nurse said, "Alyssa, Trevor, and Taryn, your turn." It was our turn. I got half dragged and I half walked. The door creaked open. It was the room of no return. The door slammed shut. There was no way out. Grown-ups guarding every outryway, making sure we couldn't escape. Seeing there was no way out we gave up and went for it.

Trevor went first. Before the shot was even touching him he was already howling. When it did hit him he was yelling loud enough to deafen you. He was done. It was my turn (he was still crying so a nurse tried to calm him down).

I was paralyzed with fear, I was death-defyed, I was scared. My mom and dad told me to "just be brave." "Just be brave?!" How could I "just be brave?!" But I had no time to think. It was coming. Just waiting to pounce, just waiting to penetrate my skin! I saw why Trevor had screamed so loud. I couldn't hear anything, I could just see it coming, closer, closer!

It touched, entered my flesh, and fufilled it's job. I started with a whimper then, BOOM! full blast cry.

When Taryn had her turn she

Score Point 4 *continued*

didn't even notice! Ugh! She was supposed to cry the most! Worse than Trevor!

But then I remembered it was over. We opened the door and the sparkling sun blinded our eyes. It was over. All over. Finally.

Score Point 4 *continued*

Assessment Summary: "Getting Shot and Living Through It"

ELEMENTS		
	Meets Standard	**Commentary**
Orientation and Context	• Orients and engages the reader (e.g., sets the time, indicates the location where the story takes place, introduces character(s), or enters immediately into the story line).	The writer orients and engages the reader by setting the scene in the opening paragraph (he and his family are sitting in the "darkness filled, mountain-top cold, waiting room" and "preparing for the shots of our lives").
Plot Development and Organization	• Creates a series of events or incidents. • Organizes the text; purposefully selects and orders events. • Paces the narrative to highlight the significance of events or incidents, to create drama or suspense, etc. • Elaborates key events, incidents, and actions, including a focal event. • Omits irrelevant incidents or events.	The story includes a series of events that are ordered purposefully (he and his family sit in the waiting room in fear; the nurse calls them back into an examining room; he sees his little brother get a shot; he gets a shot). The writer paces the narrative to create suspense by describing his dread in the waiting room and the fear he feels while he watches his brother get the first shot. He elaborates on key moments, such as his fear in the waiting room, but omits irrelevant information.
Character/Narrator Development	• Develops complex characters or provides insights about the persona of the narrator (e.g., by describing the character's or narrator's actions or internal thoughts, feelings, desires, fears).	The writer develops the persona of the first-person narrator by including information about his experiences ("I had had shots before. They were not your best friend.") and internal thoughts ("It was like knowing you would be put to sleep, sent to the dementors, waiting to take a ride in the Electric Chair.").
Closure	• Provides closure with one or more strategies (e.g., a circle story format, a reflection, a surprise ending).	The writer provides a sense of closure by describing the sunlight outside the dark, cold doctor's office and by describing his relief ("It was over. All over. Finally.").

STRATEGIES		
	Meets Standard	**Commentary**
Detail	• Uses details selectively (e.g., to describe action, create images, develop characters or persona of the narrator).	The details about the waiting room create an image of the scene ("The room was big, no, huge which gave it all the more reason to be terror bringing.").
Dialogue	• Dialogue, if present, is used purposefully (e.g., to advance the action, to develop characters or to provide background information for the reader).	The text's dialogue advances the action (the nurse calling their names), and the interior monologue helps readers understand the narrator's fear.
Other	• Uses literary language (e.g., "quick as lightning she ran away"). • Uses temporal words, phrases, and clauses to indicate shifts in time (e.g., "After a long while...").	The writer uses literary language in this piece ("dementor," a word from *Harry Potter*). The piece includes temporal words, phrases, and clauses ("Before the shot..."; "When Taryn had her turn..."; "But then I remembered..."). The writer manipulates sentence structures for effect ("Who knew what would be lurking in the corner! Rats, monsters, anything!").
Note: The commentary highlights the elements and strategies in the student paper, focusing on how well the paper addresses the totality of the elements and strategies rather than on whether each is included.		

Score Point 3

Narrative Student Work and Commentary: "On a weekend..."

On a weekend, my mom went to rent movies while my dad watched my brother and me. We were in the kitchen, running and goofing around. I started running and tickling my brother at the same time. He lost control of were he was going and his head slammed into the counter's jagged edge. Well, he started running up the stairs with me running after. Peering through his room I saw what had happened. The jagged edge of the counter sliced deep down in his head, but not to his brain at least. I saw tears rolling down his cheeks and blood dripping down the side of his head. Shocked, I ran downstairs to my dad gasping out," Jacob's bleeding, Jacob's beeding" My dad's jaw dropped down and he gasped. This was the first time I saw my dad run so fast up the stairs. Nearing my way upstairs, my dad brought Jacob to the bathroom and started putting wet-cloths to his cut and wiping the floor. We both hurriedly helped Jacob to his feet and put on his socks and shoes. I forced my socks and shoes on as my dad seriously said," Help Jake to the car while I get my socks and shoes on." I followed orders and brought Jake to the car. Dad came, turned on the car, and drove to the movie place to pick up mom. Hurt, guilty, and sad, I told mom exactly what happened. She said,"It's not your fault you accidently did that and you also told dad what happened and that was the

This young writer controls the basic series of events in this piece, but he has created what amounts to a "bed-to-bed" account of his brother's accident. The piece needs revision to develop selectivity about which events to relate and how to elaborate on them; therefore, it does not meet the standard for narrative writing.

The writer orients the reader in the first two sentences (it's the weekend, and he and his brother are home with his father). The piece would benefit from additional contextual information to set the scene and help develop reader interest (such as more information about the narrator's relationship with his brother).

Score Point 3 *continued*

right thing to do." My heart suddenly felt proud of myself. Now it was time to walk into the hospital. The nurse said, "Wait until we call your name. When we do, I'll bring you to the right room." So we waited in the waiting room. There was a T.V so that sort of entertained us. Finally our name was called and the nurse brought us to a small room. Jacob hopped onto the bed with mom next to him holding his pale hand. His face was in a frightened, pale expretion. Then the docter walked in. He asked what happened, how old he was, and asked to look at the deep bloody cut. Examining the cut he said, "He'll need some stiches, but these stiches will have to be staples." Then he walked out to get the staple stiches. Jake's face was now as white and pale as a ghost. It also seemed as if his pale hand was squeezing mom's hand to hard. The docter walked back in. He told Jake to turn his head so that the cut was facing him and told him to lye on his back. Ca ching ca ching!! Ca ching Ca ching!! The sound was horrible but not as terrible as the scream of Jake. I couldn't watch, so I hid my eyes with a magazine. The sound stopped. It was over. We walked out to our car and drove to an ice cream place. Dad said, "Who wants ice cream!"

"We do!!" Jake and I said happily. We smiled and licked our ice cream happily.

The piece includes a series of events related to Jacob's accident (Jacob hits his head; the family goes with Jacob to the hospital; the doctor gives Jacob stitches). The writer misses opportunities to dramatize and elaborate on the more significant moments in the story (such as the accident itself, the confession of guilt to his mother, and the treatment of the wound). Instead, one moment follows another, and details such as "We both hurriedly helped Jacob to his feet and put on his socks and shoes" are given equal space with moments such as "He lost control of were his was going and his head slammed into the counter's jagged edge."

The piece includes some character development, such as the description of his father's reaction to the accident ("My dad's jaw dropped and he gasped. This

Score Point 3 *continued*

I still remember this time because of how scary it was and because Jacob's scare.

was the first time I saw my dad run so fast up the stairs.") and the narrator's confession of his guilt to his mother.

The writer provides a sense of closure by describing how the family went out for ice cream when they left the hospital and by explaining the significance of the event ("I still remember this time because of how scary it was and because Jacob's scare.").

This piece includes some details to describe the character's reaction ("Jake's face was now white and pale as a ghost."), but the writer could include more details and elaborate on significant events.

The piece includes dialogue (such as the nurse asking the family to wait for her), but for the most part, the dialogue does not reveal information about the characters.

Score Point 3 *continued*

Assessment Summary: "On a weekend..."

ELEMENTS		
	Needs Revision	**Commentary**
Orientation and Context	• Orients and engages the reader (e.g., sets the time, indicates the location where the story takes place, introduces the character(s) or enters immediately into the story line).	The writer orients the reader in the first two sentences (it's the weekend, and he and his brother are home with his father). The piece would benefit from additional contextual information to set the scene and help develop reader interest (such as more information about the narrator's relationship with his brother).
Plot Development and Organization	• Creates a series of incidents or events. • Provides some pacing.	The piece includes a series of events related to Jacob's accident (Jacob hits his head; the family goes with Jacob to the hospital; the doctor gives Jacob stitches). The writer misses opportunities to dramatize and elaborate on the more significant moments in the story (such as the accident itself, the confession of guilt to his mother, and the treatment of the wound). Instead, one moment follows another, and details such as "We both hurriedly helped Jacob to his feet and put on his socks and shoes" are given equal space with moments such as "He lost control of were his was going and his head slammed into the counter's jagged edge."
Character/Narrator Development	• Includes some character development (e.g., by describing the character's or narrator's actions or internal thoughts, feelings, desires, fears).	The piece includes some character development, such as the description of his father's reaction to the accident ("My dad's jaw dropped and he gasped. This was the first time I saw my dad run so fast up the stairs.") and the narrator's confession of his guilt to his mother.
Closure	• Provides closure with one or more strategies (e.g., a circle story format, a reflection, a surprise ending).	The writer provides a sense of closure by describing how the family went out for ice cream when they left the hospital and by explaining the significance of the event ("I still remember this time because of how scary it was and because Jacob's scare.").

STRATEGIES		
	Needs Revision	**Commentary**
Detail	• Includes details, but may not use them selectively.	This piece includes some details to describe the character's reaction ("Jake's face was now white and pale as a ghost."), but the writer could include more details and elaborate on significant events.
Dialogue	• Dialogue, if present, may not be used purposefully (e.g., to advance the action, to develop characters, or to provide background information for the reader).	The piece includes dialogue (such as the nurse asking the family to wait for her), but for the most part, the dialogue does not reveal information about the characters.
Other	• May use literary language. • Uses temporal words, phrases, and clauses to indicate shifts in time.	
Note: The commentary highlights the elements and strategies in the student paper, focusing on how well the paper addresses the totality of the elements and strategies rather than on whether each is included.		

Possible Conference Topics

The writer will benefit from a conference to discuss setting the scene for readers, elaborating on significant parts of the tale, and using dialogue and interior monologue to aid in character development.

Score Point 2

Narrative Student Work and Commentary: "The Bat in the Bathroom"

The Bat in the Bathroom

I went to the delta over the summer vacation. But there is one memory that sticks out he most.

One after noon my Aunt Karen told me to take a shower. So I went to take a shower.

The bathroom was nothing special it had a sink, a toilet, and a shower with a really long curtain.

I was washing my hair when I slipped on the curtain fell; a bat woke up and flew around the room. I was terrified. I grabbed the curtain and pulled it over my head. Then I grabbed my towel. The bat flew to the opposite side of the room, behind another towel.

I started blowing on the towel. I opened the door and the bat flew out. My uncle saw it fly out.

I got changed then walked into the screen room, that's were my cousin T.J., My Uncle Justin, and Big John were. [Big John is my Uncle Justin dad.]

When I got in the screen room I sat down and told them about the bat in the bathroom. My uncle said " Oh yeah I saw it fly out of the bathroom."

After that they kept making fun of me by saying, " Can you check the bathroom for any bats." I would say " Ha! Ha very funny" They kept making fun of me till I left on Thursday.

I had lots of fun at the delta but the bat experience just scares me!

"The Bat in the Bathroom" follows the basic structure of narrative (the piece includes introductory information and a conclusion, and describes a series of events), but the piece needs significant elaboration and detail to develop the story that the writer has outlined. The author of this piece needs instruction in order to meet the standard for narrative writing.

The writer establishes a context for the piece with the opening paragraph ("I went to the delta over summer vacation. But there is one memory that sticks out the most."). The piece does not include information about where "the delta" is located, who she's traveling with, or why she's visiting.

The writer creates a series of events that occurred while the narrator was at the delta (she took a shower, saw a bat and felt scared, got teased by her uncles). The writer does not elaborate on key events (such as her encounter with the bat), and she does not

Score Point 2 *continued*

make clear connections between events (such as her summer trip and her aunt's request for her to take a shower).

The writer attempts pacing by providing more information about her encounter with the bat ("I slipped on the curtain fell; a bat woke up and flew around the room. I was terrified.").

There is a first-person narrator in this piece, but the story does not include much detail about the narrator's thoughts and feelings (such as dialogue with her aunt; internal monologue that describes her feelings about the trip, the bat, and her uncles' teasing; or description of the delta and her aunt's family).

The piece concludes with the statement "I had lots of fun at the delta but the bat experience just scares me!"

The writer provides some general information about the scene for readers (the bathroom "had a sink, a toilet, and a shower with a really long curtain").

The text includes dialogue between the narrator and her uncles ("they kept making fun of me by saying, 'Can you check the bathroom for any bats.'"), but the dialogue does not help advance the action, develop characters, or provide background information.

The piece includes temporal words, phrases, and clauses to indicate shifts in time ("When I got in the screen room..."; "After that...").

Score Point 2 *continued*

Assessment Summary: "The Bat in the Bathroom"

ELEMENTS		
	Needs Instruction	**Commentary**
Orientation and Context	• Establishes a context (e.g., time, place, or occasion). • May attempt to develop reader interest.	The writer establishes a context for the piece with the opening paragraph ("I went to the delta over summer vacation. But there is one memory that sticks out the most."). The piece does not include information about where "the delta" is located, who she's traveling with, or why she's visiting.
Plot Development and Organization	• Creates a series of incidents or events. • May not be selective in describing events. • Attempts to provide pacing.	The writer creates a series of events that occurred while the narrator was at the delta (she took a shower, saw a bat and felt scared, got teased by her uncles). The writer does not elaborate on key events (such as her encounter with the bat), and she does not make clear connections between events (such as her summer trip and her aunt's request for her to take a shower). The writer attempts pacing by providing more information about her encounter with the bat ("I slipped on the curtain fell; a bat woke up and flew around the room. I was terrified.").
Character/Narrator Development	• Includes minimal character development.	There is a first-person narrator in this piece, but the story does not include much detail about the narrator's thoughts and feelings (such as dialogue with her aunt; internal monologue that describes her feelings about the trip, the bat and her uncles' teasing; or description of the delta and her aunt's family).
Closure	• May use simple concluding statements or formal markers (e.g., "The End").	The piece concludes with the statement "I had lots of fun at the delta but the bat experience just scares me!"

Score Point 2 *continued*

STRATEGIES		
	Needs Instruction	**Commentary**
Detail	• Provides few details.	The writer provides some general information about the scene for readers (the bathroom "had a sink, a toilet, and a shower with a really long curtain").
Dialogue	• Dialogue, if present, may not be used purposefully (e.g., to advance the action, to develop characters, or to provide background information for the reader).	The text includes dialogue between the narrator and her uncles ("they kept making fun of me by saying, 'Can you check the bathroom for any bats.'"), but the dialogue does not help advance the action, develop characters, or provide background information.
Other	• May use literary language. • Uses temporal words, phrases, and clauses.	The piece includes temporal words, phrases, and clauses to indicate shifts in time ("When I got in the screen room..."; "After that...").
Note: The commentary highlights the elements and strategies in the student paper, focusing on how well the paper addresses the totality of the elements and strategies rather than on whether each is included.		

Next Steps in Instruction

The writer will benefit from instruction on filling in the skeleton of a story with information and detail so the reader can visualize place and detail, selecting and elaborating on events, developing a conclusion, and providing explicit details about places, events, and people with which she is familiar but readers are not.

Score Point 1

Narrative Student Work and Commentary: "Story of My Cut Finger"

This piece is a straightforward, if very brief, recount. The writer begins with an initiating event (cutting her finger), and then she simply recounts the events immediately following her accident. There is no attempt at development in the writing (no characterization, pacing, or sense of how the characters felt), except for the introductory "OUCH."

The writer immediately draws readers into the story line by using "OUCH" to announce her accident.

The explanation for her "OUCH" response ("I cut my finger from sharpening knives.") provides context in a limited way.

There is a recounting of events following the accident (ran to the bathroom, washed her finger, received help from her mother), but no selectivity or pacing.

There is no character development except, perhaps, a clue about a caring mother who asked to see her daughter's injury.

Score Point 1 *continued*

Story Of My Cut Finger

"OUCH" I yelled when I cut my finger
from sharpening knives. Blood was leaking
from my finger so I had to run as fast as
I could. When I got to the bathroom
I washed my finger then I helded to see if
it was still leaking. Then I put four band-
aids on, it was a little sore but I felt all
right. My mom asked me to see what happened
to me, then I showed her my finger with band-
aids. She said that I was a poor thing, and I
will never sharpen knives ever again. THE END

Closure is provided by both a summing up ("I will never sharpen knives again.") and the statement "THE END."

There are some details ("run as fast as I could," "four band-aids"), but these do not serve to develop the story.

The writer uses temporal connectives ("then," "when I got to the bathroom").

Score Point 1 *continued*

Assessment Summary: "Story of My Cut Finger"

ELEMENTS		
	Needs Substantial Support	**Commentary**
Orientation and Context	• Establishes a context (e.g., time, place, or occasion). • Typically does not develop reader interest.	The writer immediately draws readers into the story line by using "OUCH" to announce her accident. The explanation for her "OUCH" response ("I cut my finger from sharpening knives.") provides context in a limited way.
Plot Development and Organization	• Creates a series of incidents or events; typically is not selective in describing events. • Provides a simple recounting of events or incidents with no pacing.	There is a recounting of events following the accident (ran to the bathroom, washed her finger, received help from her mother), but no selectivity or pacing.
Character/Narrator Development	• Includes little or no character development.	There is no character development except, perhaps, a clue about a caring mother who asked to see her daughter's injury.
Closure	• May use simple concluding statements or formal markers (e.g., "The End").	Closure is provided by both a summing up ("I will never sharpen knives again.") and the statement "THE END."
STRATEGIES		
	Needs Substantial Support	**Commentary**
Detail	• Provides few details.	There are some details ("run as fast as I could," "four band-aids"), but these do not serve to develop the story.
Dialogue	• Dialogue, if present, typically is not used purposefully (e.g., to advance the action, to develop characters, or to provide background information for the reader).	
Other	• May use literary language. • Uses temporal words, phrases, and clauses.	The writer uses temporal connectives ("then," "when I got to the bathroom").

Note: The commentary highlights the elements and strategies in the student paper, focusing on how well the paper addresses the totality of the elements and strategies rather than on whether each is included.

Roadmap for Development

The writer needs instruction and practice in developing a "story" rather than a simple recount. There is nothing fundamentally wrong with the piece; it is simply undeveloped. However, any piece of writing this brief suggests that some development of fluency should be an instructional first step. The student should also receive instruction on using detail to flesh out characters and events.

Report of Information

Reports of information describe the way things are in the social and natural world. They describe classes of things, but also the components or parts of things and their relations. Reports contain various kinds of information. They answer questions such as, What are the major food groups? What is the earth made of? What role do planets play in the solar system? Reports also give information about aspects of things. They answer questions about size (How big is Texas? How tall is the Eiffel Tower?), about function (What is a telescope used for? What is a modem used for?), about behavior (What do pelicans do to find food? How do whales eat?), and about the organization of systems (What is the relationship of the House to the Senate? How is the court system organized?). Writers of this genre typically make meaning by describing and classifying things and their distinctive features. For children, this often means writing about the features of different kinds of dinosaurs, insects, planes, pets, whales, and so on. When children study science, their reports may deal with different kinds of energy, different kinds of clouds, different types of cells, etc.

Report writing poses many challenges for young students. Writing about a topic that they know well presents a different set of challenges than writing about a topic that is unfamiliar. When students know the topic, organizing the information is the primary task that consumes their energy. When they do not know the topic, gathering and phrasing the information present additional challenges.

When students are writing about a topic they are familiar with, they can convey information in their own words and cluster information in categories that make sense to them. When they do not know the topic, they may not have the breadth or depth of understanding to analyze and categorize the information effectively. In these cases, young writers often seem to rely almost solely on headers, provided either by the teacher or by the reference materials themselves, to organize their writing.

When students do not know the topic, simply phrasing the information can be a daunting task. They must explain new information that they may not fully understand. So, the logical thing for them to do is to borrow heavily from the wording in reference books to make sure they convey correctly the ideas they are writing about. Logically, then, the syntactic patterns that emerge under these circumstances frequently are made up of some introductory, transitional, or evaluative phrasings that string together word-for-word borrowings from reference books. This is called "patch" writing and it is particularly acceptable and expected in the primary grades, where students are encouraged to mimic the language of written texts, to apprentice themselves to authors and to borrow stylistic techniques they observe professional writers using.

The New Standards expectation for student writers in the report genre requires that they be able to craft a report that does the following: establishes a context; creates an organizing structure appropriate to audience and purpose; communicates ideas, insights, or theories that are illustrated through facts, details, quotations, statistics, and other information; uses a range of appropriate strategies to develop the text; and provides closure.

Orientation and Context

As it relates to report writing, orienting the reader usually means providing some kind of opening statement locating the subject of the paper in the universe of things. For children, the opening statement often takes the form of a definition or classification ("Whales are mammals."). Alternatively, opening statements will sometimes provide an overview of the topic ("There are many different types of whales in the ocean.") or a comment on the organization of a system ("There are three branches in the government of the United States."). Young writers also often attempt to engage reader interest in the topic by introducing startling facts or by appealing to the reader in some fashion.

Organization of Information

In reports, facts are often grouped into topic areas in a hierarchical pattern of organization such as classification. Reports also describe patterns of relations among concepts linked to facts. Although reports are often considered neutral and voiceless, in reality they convey human agendas or points of view. Thus, effective reports have a controlling idea or perspective that contributes to the organization and coherence of the text. That is, information is selected and ordered in a way that contributes to the development of the idea. Organizing information in a report also requires writers to attend to the needs of their audience by providing the background information a reader would need to understand subsequent portions of the text. Writers also use paragraphing, subheads, transition words, and phrases and clauses to organize the information.

Development and Specificity of Information

There is a wide variety of ways to report information. Writers define things ("Corn is a vegetable."), give examples ("Dogs are man's best friend. Guide dogs help blind people."), and provide reasons ("My mom works on computers...I know why, she's an engineer."). Writers also explain phenomena ("Atoms are the insides of crystals.... Crystals get flat faces because the atoms form regular patterns inside."). They compare ("Some crystals are like flowers."; "Gray rabbits look like ash and smoke.") and they contrast ("Some crystals grow from lava and some grow from sea salt."). They relate cause and effect ("We used to have a dog, but my dad left the door open and he ran out into the street."). They describe ("Dolphins have a sharp and pointed face."). They specify ("I learned a lot from doing this report. I learned about different types of dogs and breeds."). They evaluate ("All crystals are different and that's what makes them so wonderful."). The different strategies that writers use can vary from a single sentence to a chunk of text several sentences long.

In developing information in a report, effective writers provide adequate and specific information about the topic. They usually write in the present tense and exclude information that is extraneous or inappropriate. They communicate ideas, insights, and theories that are elaborated on or illustrated by facts, details, quotations, statistics, or other information. Their language is factual and precise, rather than general and non-specific. They use clear and precise descriptive language to convey distinctive features (such as shape, size, color), components (such as parts of a machine, players on a team), behaviors (such as behaviors of animals: birthing, mating, eating), uses (such as uses of soap: washing hair, washing clothes, washing cars). Frequently, writers use specialized vocabulary specifically related to the topic (such as "pride," "cubs," and "dominant male" in a paper about lion families).

Many young writers pick topics from their everyday lives that they are knowledgeable about and that lend themselves to everyday vocabulary (such as siblings, family members, the family dog). In these cases, the writing may appear less sophisticated than the writing of a student who has picked a topic that lends itself to the use of technical vocabulary. But when students work with less familiar topics, the language they use may not appear to be their own. Both situations, in their own way, make it difficult to accurately evaluate the writer's development. It is important to keep in mind, though, that young writers who are imitating the language of the books they read are in the process of making that language their own.

Closure

Although their reports may not always have a formal conclusion, as would be expected in the writing of adults, young writers typically provide some sort of closure, such as a shift from particular facts to some kind of general statement or claim about the topic ("Everything is an adventure when you have a passport. All you have to do is get one!").

Report of Information in Fifth Grade

By fifth grade, students should have had a good deal of experience reading informational texts and writing reports. Nevertheless, some students will still be struggling with the challenges this genre presents. Like struggling writers in earlier grades, they may find it difficult to analyze and categorize information. They may cluster details, but fail to organize them in a way that supports a controlling idea or perspective on the subject. They may use a simple list or other loose organizational structure to present information. Although they may develop information around a topic, the information may not be adequate. For instance, a writer might describe the rules of a game, but not the game itself. Struggling writers may also have difficulty gathering adequate information about their topic and, in turn, are unable to convey a knowledgeable stance. Some young writers may even comment explicitly on what they do not know ("What I don't know is for how long.") along with what they know. These students lag behind expectations for report writing at fifth grade.

Writers who meet the standard for report writing at fifth grade communicate elaborated ideas, insights, or theories through facts, concrete details, quotations, statistics, or other information in support of a controlling idea or perspective on the subject (for example, "California is a diverse state."; "Training a guide dog can be challenging and rewarding."). They create effective organizing structures appropriate for their purposes. For instance, one young writer who was reporting on the training of guide dogs provided transition words to signal milestones in the training process ("When a guide dog puppy is three months old..."; "When the dog has to go back to the training school..."; "The first days at the school..."; "Within a few days..."; "When the dog passes..."). Although their vocabulary may not be highly technical if the topic does not warrant it, writers who meet expectations at this grade level use specialized vocabulary related to the topic ("veterinarian," "harness," "kennel," "trainer," "basic obedience").

In general, however, writers who meet the standard at this grade level employ advanced vocabulary and syntax compared to the vocabulary and syntax of writers who do not meet the standard. They use a variety of strategies to convey information, give examples ("It learns to sit, lie down, stay and to greet visitors nicely."), provide adequate and specific facts and information ("The puppy lives with the family from the time it is two or three months old until it is a year or year and a half old."), and generalize ("All dogs that are chosen for training must have the qualities needed to be a good guide dog."). They have a wide repertoire of strategies for report writing and demonstrate flexibility in their use.

Report of Information Rubrics Elements

	5 Exceeds Standard*	4 Meets Standard
Orientation and Context	• Introduces the topic. • Engages the reader and develops reader interest. • Establishes a context. • Conveys a knowledgeable stance.	• Introduces the topic. • Engages the reader and develops reader interest. • Establishes a context. • Conveys a knowledgeable stance.
Organization of Information	• Develops a controlling idea or perspective on the subject (e.g., "Alligators are awesome."). • Creates an effective organizing structure. • Orders information effectively, providing background information needed to understand subsequent portions of the text.	• Develops a controlling idea or perspective on the subject (e.g., "Alligators are awesome."). • Creates an effective organizing structure. • Orders information effectively, providing background information needed to understand subsequent portions of the text.
Development and Specificity of Information	• Reports well-developed and specific facts and information pertinent to the topic. • Communicates elaborated ideas, insights, or theories through facts, concrete details, quotations, statistics, or other information in support of the controlling idea or perspective.	• Reports well-developed and specific facts and information pertinent to the topic. • Communicates elaborated ideas, insights, or theories through facts, concrete details, quotations, statistics, or other information in support of the controlling idea or perspective.
Closure	• Provides a conclusion.	• Provides a conclusion.

	3 Needs Revision	2 Needs Instruction	1 Needs Substantial Support
Orientation and Context	• Introduces the topic. • Engages the reader and develops reader interest. • May establish a context. • May convey a knowledgeable stance.	• Introduces the topic. • Attempts to engage the reader. • May establish a context.	• Introduces the topic. • May attempt to engage the reader. • Typically does not establish a context.
Organization of Information	• Develops a controlling idea or perspective on the subject (e.g., "Alligators are awesome."). • Clusters details in an organizing structure.	• Conveys a perspective. • Clusters details in an organizing structure.	• May create a simple list or use a loose organizational structure.
Development and Specificity of Information	• Develops information and reports on a topic, but may lack adequate and specific facts and information pertinent to the topic.	• Develops information and reports on a topic, but may lack adequate and specific facts and information pertinent to the topic.	• Develops information and reports on a topic, but typically lacks adequate and specific facts and information pertinent to the topic.
Closure	• Provides a conclusion.	• Typically provides a conclusion or concluding statement.	• Typically provides a conclusion or concluding statement.

*The criteria that define score points 5 and 4 are identical. This is intentional. What distinguishes a 5 from a 4 is not the presence or absence of a particular element or strategy. Rather it is the overall quality of execution and the level of language the writer employs. Writers of score point 5 papers bring something to the text that may not be provided by instruction—a deep understanding or passion for the topic and the genre.

Report of Information Rubrics Strategies

	5 Exceeds Standard*	4 Meets Standard
Names and Vocabulary	• Uses names and specialized vocabulary specific to the topic.	• Uses names and specialized vocabulary specific to the topic.
Other	• May include illustrations or graphics to support the text. • Employs a straightforward tone.	• May include illustrations or graphics to support the text. • Employs a straightforward tone.

	3 Needs Revision	2 Needs Instruction	1 Needs Substantial Support
Names and Vocabulary	• Uses names and specialized vocabulary specific to the topic.	• Uses names and specialized vocabulary related to the topic.	• May use names and specialized vocabulary related to the topic.
Other	• May include illustrations or graphics to support the text. • Employs a straightforward tone.	• May include illustrations or graphics to support the text. • Employs a straightforward tone.	• May include illustrations or graphics to support the text. • Employs a straightforward tone.

*The criteria that define score points 5 and 4 are identical. This is intentional. What distinguishes a 5 from a 4 is not the presence or absence of a particular element or strategy. Rather, it is the overall quality of execution and the level of language the writer employs. Writers of score point 5 papers bring something to the text that may not be provided by instruction—a deep understanding or passion for the topic and the genre.

Score Point 5

Report of Information Student Work and Commentary: "The Life of a Guide Dog Puppy"

The first time I really got interested in guide dogs was when I was at school. I was watching a play and one of the characters had a guide dog. I realized that without the dog the person would not be able to go places. So two years later I decided to do my report on guide dogs because I was interested in them. I started by looking on the internet. I wanted to know how guide dogs are trained from beginning to end. It takes two years for guide dog puppies to be taught to guide. Between the ages, six and eleven the puppies are tested once a week. If a dog is very cautious or easily scared it might not make a good guide dog. Guide dog schools only train German shepherds, golden retrievers and Labrador retrievers. Why do they only train these dogs? Because they are intelligent and enjoy working with people. All dogs that are chosen for training must have the qualities needed to be a good guide dog. The dogs must be strong, be intelligent, and be kind.

After I got some info on the computer I started to hi light the info. A few days later I went to the public library. I looked for books on guide dogs. When I was looking in a book I saw something about donating your dog, but why would someone want to donate their dog?

When a guide dog puppy is three months old it goes to live with a family that has volunteered to help raise the puppy. Why would the school need help from a family that they don't really know. Many families are in a club called 4H. To be a guide dog puppy raiser, you need to fill out an application. After the application is looked over the puppy placement department gives you a packet on care and also a chart to record the dog's growth. They also give you a dog collar showing the telephone number of the training school, and the dog's identification number just in case the dog gets lost. The puppy lives with the family from the time it is two or three months old until it is a year or year and a half old. Does the dog have to be on good behavior all the time. The puppy becomes one of the family at the same time, it learns not to beg for food or make pee puddles on the floor. It learns to sit, lie down, stay and to greet visitors nicely. This training is called "basic obedience". My dog would never be able to do that because she's too stupid. The dog learns it's way up and down the city streets and country roads. That's a lot to learn for a dog. It rides in cars and on buses. The dog gets used to all kinds of family activities and learns to adapt easily to a variety of different things, and this will help it adapt to a blind person's life style. A puppy raiser is responsible for the care of their dog during the time they have the dog. They must house train and feed the puppy and keep it clean and healthy. An important part of being a puppy raiser is getting the dog use to going out into the community because this will be the dog's job when it is working with a blind person. It must be hard to train a guide dog.

"The Life of a Guide Dog Puppy" includes specific and detailed information about how guide dogs are raised and trained. This paper exceeds the standard for informational writing at fifth grade.

The writer introduces the topic and engages the reader by opening his paper with a personal anecdote about when and how he first became interested in guide dogs ("I was watching a play and one of the characters had a guide dog.").

The writer announces the piece's controlling idea in the first paragraph ("I wanted to know how guide dogs are trained from beginning to end."). He provides a detailed preview of the training process in the introduction, relating information about the kinds

Score Point 5 *continued*

When the dog has to go back to the training school it is sometimes hard for the family to give the dog up. Even though the family has known from the start that it was raising the dog to become an important part of a blind person's life it must be hard giving up a dog that you have become attached to. Many families raise several guide dog puppies. Getting a new puppy makes it a bit easier to give one up to the guide dog school. When the puppy comes back to the school it goes through a lot of examinations. The instructor checks the dog over and measures the dog's height and weight. The veterinarian gives the dog a throat examination and x-rays the dog. The veterinarian wants to make sure the dog does not develop any problems that would prevent him from walking properly. That's a lot of things the vet has to do.

The first days at the school may be hard for the young dog. Within a few days the dog trainer becomes it's new best friend. Dogs really do get attached to people fast. The two are together most of the time, at the kennel, and sometimes at the trainer's house. Soon the dog is having a fine time playing "training games". Training is always made fun. I wonder what training games are? A guide dog has to like it's work. During training the dog gets used to wearing a harness. With the harness around the dog's body the dog is taught to pull forward while walking on the left side and ahead of the trainer. It usually takes a guide dog several days to learn to stop at each curb and wait for a command, to go forward or to turn. Training a guide dog is a lot more complicated than I thought.

If the dog doesn't pass it's final test the dog would not be able to offered to a blind person. But the dog still makes a great pet. The raiser has the first chance to adopt the dog, but if for some reason the raiser doesn't want the dog it will be offered to someone else. Only about half the dogs complete every stage of training and become a guide dog.

It takes skilled dog trainers to train guide dogs but volunteers are the key to the school's success. What do volunteers do? A guide dog is usually able to pass the test with the help of volunteers. The volunteers help train the guide dogs and work in kennels. They also help the trainers keep records. I never knew that volunteers would be so helpful to the program. They also help clean the floors, care for newborn puppies, feed and clean and exercise the dogs. Wow! Volunteers really are the key to the school's success.

Three times a day all the dogs are let out into a large fenced area where the dogs can run and exercise. This gives the dogs a chance to get to know each other. Guide dogs must be comfortable around other animals so they do not become afraid or mean.

In order for the dog to complete all tests it must go through the last step of training. The final part of the dog's training is when the trainer asks the dog to lead her on the sidewalk. This time the trainer's eyes are covered. When the dog passes it will be matched up to a blind person.

The blind person lives at the school for a few weeks where they learn to work with their dogs. The guide dog and the blind person become great friends and hardly are ever apart. The guide dog has to retire when it is ten, eleven or

of breeds that are trained, the qualities a guide dog needs, and the length of the training process. The writer conveys a knowledgeable stance by describing in detail each step in the training process.

The text is organized chronologically to explain the process of training a puppy to guide, from placement with a family at 3 months of age through the final steps when the dog passes its tests and a blind person comes to the school to learn to work with the dog. The writer also uses transition devices to indicate potential interruptions in the sequence, as well as conditions that must be met ("If the dog doesn't pass it's final test..."). The writer also uses questions that readers might ask as a device to organize his text ("Why do they only train these dogs?" and "Why would the school need help from a family that they don't really know.").

The information provided is frequently quite specific. For instance, the writer specifically names the only breeds of dogs that are trained as guide dogs: "German shepherds, golden retrievers and Labrador retrievers." He describes each element of the veterinarian's

Score Point 5 *continued*

twelve years old.

It takes thousands of dollars to train a guide dog. However, blind people may get a dog for very little money or sometimes for free. Guide dog schools get their money from private foundations, businesses and other sponsors.

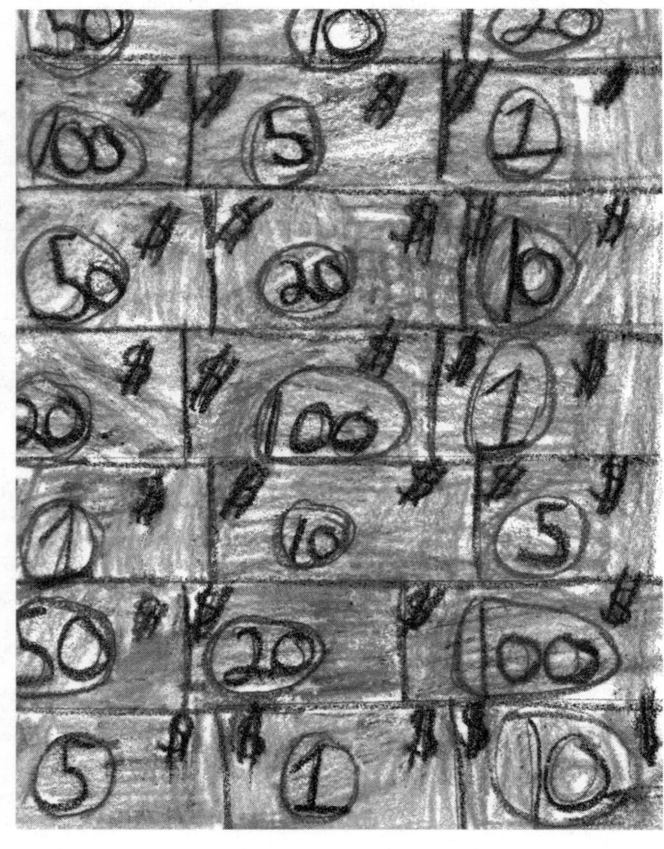

examination and specifies the number of times a day the dogs are let out to exercise at the school.

He supports the perspective he has on the subject, that the training process is thorough, complicated, and intensive and that guide dogs must "be strong, be intelligent, and be kind," with numerous details and explanations. He explains, for instance, that it takes intelligence for a puppy to successfully navigate basic obedience training while living with a volunteer family, and he comments, "My dog would never be able to do that because she's too stupid." His explanation is complemented by many examples of the things a dog learns while it lives with a volunteer family. He comments that the training is complicated ("Training a guide dog is a lot more complicated than I thought."), and he provides examples of the complex maneuvers guide dogs must learn ("With the harness around the dog's body the dog is taught to pull forward while walking on the left side and ahead of the trainer.").

The writer also conveys the idea that being a volunteer in the training can be challenging and rewarding. For instance, he explains that volunteer

Score Point 5 *continued*

families take on a serious responsibility when they are accepted into the training program, describing how difficult it can be to give up the dog when it has to go back to the training school and commenting, "It must be hard to train a guide dog."

Stepping back from his detailed description of the training process, the writer concludes with general comments about the cost of guide dogs and the financing for the training schools.

The writer uses names and specialized vocabulary throughout the piece ("basic obedience," "private foundations, businesses and other sponsors," and "a club called 4H").

The writer employs a straightforward tone.

Assessment Summary: "The Life of a Guide Dog Puppy"

ELEMENTS		
	Exceeds Standard	**Commentary**
Orientation and Context	• Introduces the topic. • Engages the reader and develops reader interest. • Establishes a context. • Conveys a knowledgeable stance.	The writer introduces the topic and engages the reader by opening his paper with a personal anecdote about when and how he first became interested in guide dogs ("I was watching a play and one of the characters had a guide dog."). The writer conveys a knowledgeable stance by describing in detail each step in the dog's training process.
Organization of Information	• Develops a controlling idea or perspective on the subject (e.g., "Alligators are awesome."). • Creates an effective organizing structure. • Orders information effectively, providing background information needed to understand subsequent portions of the text.	The writer announces the piece's controlling idea in the first paragraph ("I wanted to know how guide dogs are trained from beginning to end."). He provides a detailed preview of the training process in the introduction, relating information about the kinds of breeds that are trained, the qualities a guide dog needs, and the length of the training process. The remainder of the text is organized chronologically to explain the process of training a puppy to guide, from placement with a family at 3 months of age through the final steps when the dog passes its tests and a blind person comes to the school to learn to work with the dog. The writer also uses transition devices to indicate potential interruptions in the sequence, as well as conditions that must be met ("If the dog doesn't pass it's final test..."). The writer also uses questions that readers might ask as a device to organize his text ("Why do they only train these dogs?" and "Why would the school need help from a family that they don't really know.").
Development and Specificity of Information	• Reports well-developed and specific facts and information pertinent to the topic. • Communicates elaborated ideas, insights, or theories through facts, concrete details, quotations, statistics, or other information in support of the controlling idea or perspective.	The information provided is frequently quite specific. For instance, the writer specifically names the only breeds of dogs that are trained as guide dogs: "German shepherds, golden retrievers and Labrador retrievers." He describes each element of the veterinarian's examination, and he specifies the number of times a day the dogs are let out to exercise at the school. He supports the perspective he has on the subject, that the training process is thorough, complicated, and intensive and that guide dogs must "be strong, be intelligent, and be kind," with numerous details and explanations. He explains, for instance, that it takes intelligence for a puppy to successfully navigate basic obedience training while living with a volunteer family, and he comments, "My dog would never be able to do that because she's too stupid." His explanation is complemented by many examples of the things a dog learns while it lives with a volunteer family. He comments that the training is complicated ("Training a guide dog is a lot more complicated than I thought."), and he provides examples of the complex maneuvers guide dogs must learn ("With the harness around the dog's body the dog is taught to pull forward while walking on the left side and ahead of the trainer."). The writer also conveys the idea that being a volunteer in the training can be challenging and rewarding. For instance, he explains that volunteer families take on a serious responsibility when they are accepted into the training program, describing how difficult it can be to give up the dog when it has to go back to the training school and commenting, "It must be hard to train a guide dog."
Closure	• Provides a conclusion.	Stepping back from his detailed description of the training process, the writer concludes with general comments about the cost of guide dogs and the financing for the training schools.

Score Point 5 *continued*

STRATEGIES		
	Exceeds Standard	**Commentary**
Names and Vocabulary	• Uses names and specialized vocabulary specific to the topic.	The writer uses names and specialized vocabulary throughout the piece ("basic obedience," "private foundations, businesses and other sponsors," and "a club called 4H").
Other	• May include illustrations or graphics to support the text. • Employs a straightforward tone.	The writer employs a straightforward tone.
Note: The commentary highlights the elements and strategies in the student paper, focusing on how well the paper addresses the totality of the elements and strategies rather than on whether each is included.		

Score Point 4

Report of Information Student Work and Commentary: "Lion Families"

Lion Families

Imagine lion cubs playing together. Their mother is on a hunt, so an aunt guards the cubs. It's late in the afternoon and the cubs are all getting hungry. The older lions in the pride are hungry, too, especially the cubs' father. He is an old, dominant male and he needs food to keep strong to protect his pride.

My report is about lion prides and how the different animals in the pride work together. The first time I learned about lion prides was when I saw a program on Animal Planet. The program was called Prides and it told about the dominant male, the many females and their cubs, and how they all have different jobs to work together like a family. I got very interested to learn more.

Rank in a pride is very important. There is always a dominant male. He is the leader of the pride and so he is treated with a lot of respect. The dominant male always eats first at mealtime. If he's especially hungry he may eat the whole meal instead of sharing. The jobs of the dominant male are to protect the pride from other males and to mate with the females to produce new offspring.

The next most important members of the pride are the adult females. Adult females provide food for the pride. They are hunters. They also take care of the cubs in the pride. They teach them and protect them.

"Lion Families" describes interactions between different members of the lion family. This well-organized piece includes a great deal of elaborated information about the members of a lion pride and meets the standard for a fifth-grade report of information.

The writer introduces the topic, engages the reader, and establishes a context by asking readers to "imagine" a lion family in the late afternoon ("Imagine lion cubs playing together. Their mother is on a hunt, so an aunt guards the cubs.").

The writer continues by clearly stating the piece's controlling idea ("My report is about lion prides and how the different animals in the pride work together.").

The writer conveys a knowledgeable stance by using specialized vocabulary related to the topic ("The program was called Prides and it told about the dominant male, the many females and their cubs, and

Score Point 4 *continued*

Cubs are the least important members of the pride. They eat last and have to share the left over scrap that the adults leave behind. If a cub tried to eat with the adults it would get punished. When the cubs are three years old, most of them leave their pride. They either leave on their own or are forced out. Some females are allowed to stay but all the makes have to leave and live on their own until they can claim a pride of their own.

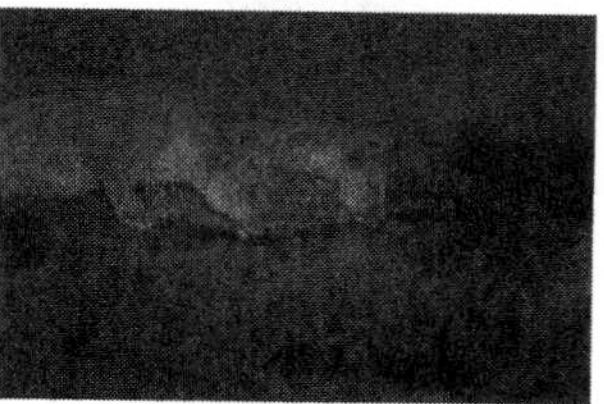

Prides also have some outcasts from other prides. These outcasts are lionesses that are not related in any way to the other members of the pride. The dominant male ignores the outcasts and won't even eat with them.

Members of the pride do not always get along. Some times both the adults and the cubs fight. Some fights are about silly things and are just for fun. But other fights are very serious. Female lions can fight over who gets to lead a hunt. They also fight when one lioness steals another female's cubs. Males fight over dominance or over who gets to mate with the females.

The lion family works pretty well. The cubs are fed and protected until they are able to go off on their own. The female lionesses hunt, feed, and teach the cubs. They produce off spring and feed the rest of the pride. The dominant male protects the pride and keeps his family together.

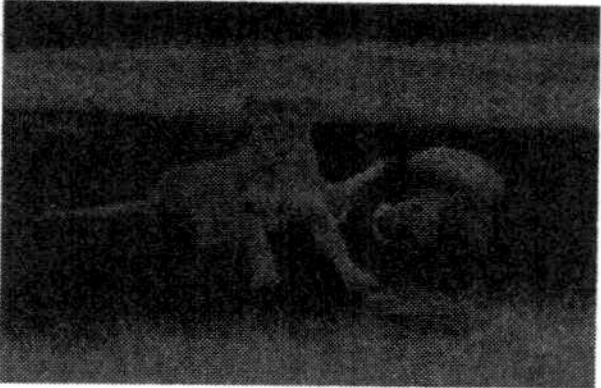

how they all have different jobs to work together like a family.").

The writer organizes the paper by discussing the "rank" and roles of the different members of the pride (dominant male, adult females, cubs, outcasts from other prides, whole-family interaction).

The information presented is well developed, and the writer elaborates on the statements she presents. For instance, the sentence "Cubs are the least important members of the pride" is supported by several examples, such as "They eat last" and a cub that breaks the rules "would get punished."

The piece concludes by explaining why the "lion family works pretty well."

The piece includes names and vocabulary specific to the topic ("dominant male," "pride," "cub," "outcasts," and "offspring").

The writer employs a straightforward tone.

Assessment Summary: "Lion Families"

ELEMENTS		
	Meets Standard	**Commentary**
Orientation and Context	• Introduces the topic. • Engages the reader and develops reader interest. • Establishes a context. • Conveys a knowledgeable stance.	The writer introduces the topic, engages the reader, and establishes a context by asking readers to "imagine" a lion family in the late afternoon ("Imagine lion cubs playing together. Their mother is on a hunt, so an aunt guards the cubs."). The writer conveys a knowledgeable stance by using specialized vocabulary related to the topic ("The program was called Prides and it told about the dominant male, the many females and their cubs, and how they all have different jobs to work together like a family.").
Organization of Information	• Develops a controlling idea or perspective on the subject (e.g., "Alligators are awesome."). • Creates an effective organizing structure. • Orders information effectively, providing background information needed to understand subsequent portions of the text.	The writer clearly states the piece's controlling idea ("My report is about lion prides and how the different animals in the pride work together."). The writer organizes the paper by discussing the "rank" and roles of the different members of the pride (dominant male, adult females, cubs, outcasts from other prides, whole-family interaction).
Development and Specificity of Information	• Reports well-developed and specific facts and information pertinent to the topic. • Communicates elaborated ideas, insights, or theories through facts, concrete details, quotations, statistics, or other information in support of the controlling idea or perspective.	The information presented is well developed, and the writer elaborates on the statements she presents. For instance, the sentence "Cubs are the least important members of the pride" is supported by several examples, such as "They eat last" and a cub that breaks the rules "would get punished."
Closure	• Provides a conclusion.	The piece concludes by explaining why the "lion family works pretty well."
STRATEGIES		
	Meets Standard	**Commentary**
Names and Vocabulary	• Uses names and specialized vocabulary specific to the topic.	The piece includes names and vocabulary specific to the topic ("dominant male," "pride," "cub," "outcasts," and "offspring").
Other	• May include illustrations or graphics to support the text. • Employs a straightforward tone.	The writer employs a straightforward tone.

Note: The commentary highlights the elements and strategies in the student paper, focusing on how well the paper addresses the totality of the elements and strategies rather than on whether each is included.

Score Point 3

Report of Information Student Work and Commentary: "Tornadoes"

TORNADOES

What a beautiful typical day on this farm. Suddenly out of nowhere formed a tunnel in the sky. This tunnel that is being formed is also called a tornado, twister, or a cyclone. As the tornado reaches to the ground gray clouds close in forming great wind blowing down. As the tornado reaches to the ground it lets go and now the beautiful farm is nothing, but wood.

How are they formed? Tornadoes are formed by hot air rising and cold air hitting against, making it to collided together. As the hot air and cold air collided, together they form a spiral that if it touches the ground it will let go and destroy anything in its path.

Where are they found? Tornadoes are found in the Midwest and southwest of the United States. Another place tornadoes happen a lot is, Tornado Ally. Tornado Ally is like a dessert, but not a dessert. Tornado Ally is hot and cold at the same time. You won't see a tornado everyday, but maybe once a month.

Tornadoes are the most destructive storms because thunderstorms harm and maybe just maybe kill somebody; unlike tornadoes they easily kill someone. Hurricanes can damage homes, but the tornado rips apart homes. Avalanches can kill and destroy many homes like the tornado, but tornadoes happen all year around and avalanches only happen in the snow; snow only comes once a year. The safest place to be during a tornado is a bathroom. Bathrooms are the safest place because all the things in a bathroom are stuck to the wall.

In "Tornadoes," the writer provides readers with information about tornadoes, such as how they are formed, where they are found, and what to do if you find yourself in the middle of one. Although the piece includes many elements of a report, in many places the writer does not provide specific information or evidence to support his claim. This piece approaches but does not meet the standard for fifth grade.

The writer of "Tornadoes" introduces the topic and engages the reader with a dramatization of the destructive power of a tornado touchdown in which a "beautiful farm" becomes "nothing, but wood." Embedded in this dramatic introduction is a definition of the topic: "a tunnel in the sky," also called "a tornado, twister, or a cyclone."

The details and explanations provided by the writer convey a knowledgeable stance. He explains, for instance, that hot air and cold air colliding form the spiral of a tornado, and he explains that tornadoes happen more frequently in some parts of the United States than others.

Following the introduction, the writer partially organizes the text around questions. In the first paragraph, he asks and answers the question "How are they formed?" In the second paragraph, the writer asks and answers the question "Where are they

Score Point 3 *continued*

The farm that was destroyed lived somewhere tornadoes happen. So remember that if tornadoes are somewhere near you you now known where to protect yourself.

found?" In the third paragraph, the writer attempts to establish the idea that tornadoes are more destructive than thunderstorms, hurricanes, and avalanches, and he offers the advice that the safest place to be when a tornado strikes is in the bathroom. In the final paragraph, he again mentions the farm destroyed by a tornado to make the point that you have to "know where to protect yourself" if you live in a place where "tornadoes happen."

The writer adopts a knowledgeable stance and provides some appropriate details and facts, but the piece is not well developed overall. The answers to the questions he asks are brief and relatively unelaborated, and the claims he makes are unsupported. For instance, the writer claims that if a tornado touches the ground, "it will let go and destroy anything in its path." The writer does not provide specifics about tornadoes that explain their destructive power, such as their wind speed, width, or ground speed. Similarly, the writer claims that tornadoes are more destructive than thunderstorms, hurricanes, and avalanches, but he fails to produce adequate support for his claim. Also, some of the information the writer provides is misleading.

The piece concludes with a reminder to readers: "So remember that if tornadoes are somewhere near you you now known where to protect yourself."

The piece includes a specific name ("Tornado Ally") and some vocabulary specifically related to the topic ("twister," "cyclone," "spiral").

The writer employs a straightforward tone.

Assessment Summary: "Tornadoes"

ELEMENTS		
	Needs Revision	**Commentary**
Orientation and Context	• Introduces the topic. • Engages the reader and develops reader interest. • May establish a context. • May convey a knowledgeable stance.	The writer of "Tornadoes" introduces the topic and engages the reader with a dramatization of the destructive power of a tornado touchdown in which a "beautiful farm" becomes "nothing, but wood." Embedded in this dramatic introduction is a definition of the topic: "a tunnel in the sky," also called "a tornado, twister, or a cyclone." The details and explanations provided by the writer convey a knowledgeable stance. He explains, for instance, that hot air and cold air colliding form the spiral of a tornado, and he explains that tornadoes happen more frequently in some parts of the United States than others.
Organization of Information	• Develops a controlling idea or perspective on the subject (e.g., "Alligators are awesome."). • Clusters details in an organizing structure.	Following the introduction, the writer partially organizes the text around questions. In the first paragraph, he asks and answers the question "How are they formed?" In the second paragraph, the writer asks and answers the question "Where are they found?" In the third paragraph, the writer attempts to establish the idea that tornadoes are more destructive than thunderstorms, hurricanes, and avalanches, and he offers the advice that the safest place to be when a tornado strikes is in the bathroom. In the final paragraph, he again mentions the farm destroyed by a tornado to make the point that you have to "know where to protect yourself" if you live in a place where "tornadoes happen."
Development and Specificity of Information	• Develops information and reports on a topic, but may lack adequate and specific facts and information pertinent to the topic.	The writer adopts a knowledgeable stance and provides some appropriate details and facts, but the piece is not well developed overall. The answers to the questions he asks are brief and relatively unelaborated, and the claims he makes are unsupported. For instance, the writer claims that if a tornado touches the ground, "it will let go and destroy anything in its path." The writer does not provide specifics about tornadoes that explain their destructive power, such as their wind speed, width, or ground speed. Similarly, the writer claims that tornadoes are more destructive than thunderstorms, hurricanes, and avalanches, but he fails to produce adequate support for his claim. Also, some of the information the writer provides is misleading.
Closure	• Provides a conclusion.	The piece concludes with a reminder to readers: "So remember that if tornadoes are somewhere near you you now known where to protect yourself."

Score Point 3 *continued*

STRATEGIES		
	Needs Revision	**Commentary**
Names and Vocabulary	• Uses names and specialized vocabulary specific to the topic.	The piece includes a specific name ("Tornado Ally") and some vocabulary specifically related to the topic ("twister," "cyclone," "spiral").
Other	• May include illustrations or graphics to support the text. • Employs a straightforward tone.	The writer employs a straightforward tone.
Note: The commentary highlights the elements and strategies in the student paper, focusing on how well the paper addresses the totality of the elements and strategies rather than on whether each is included.		

Possible Conference Topics

The writer will benefit from a conference to discuss supporting assertions with evidence, providing adequate and specific information about a topic, and elaborating on and developing information and ideas.

Score Point 2

Report of Information Student Work and Commentary: "Rules of Hockey"

Rules of Hockey

Hockey is the fastest team sport in the world It is a fun game too. I started playing hockey when I was 8 years old. I started playing hockey because I saw my older cousin playing hockey when my dad went to play soccer at Hoover School.

There are a lot of rules for Hckey. Hockey is played

In "Rules of Hockey," the writer explains the rules of the game to readers. Although he includes information about the rules of the game, the piece does not include an effective organizing structure, and throughout the piece the writer tells readers the information that he does not know about hockey. This writer will need instruction in order to meet the standard for fifth grade.

The writer introduces and attempts to engage the reader's interest by asserting that hockey is unique ("Hockey is the fastest team sport in the world."). He relates his personal experience as a hockey player, saying, "I started playing hockey when I was 8 years old."

The writer's perspective on the subject is that hockey "is the fastest team sport" and "a fun game too."

The writer develops information about the topic by explaining various rules, such as how many players play on each side, how many substitutes can be made, how long they play, the procedure for starting the game, how the games are refereed, etc. Facts and details are loosely clustered around these topics ("The hockey players play for three 20-minute periods. Sometimes I play three 20-minute periods."), but the writer does not describe the game itself.

Instead of establishing a knowledgeable stance, the writer frequently comments on what he does

Score Point 2 *continued*

6 to a side with 3 fowards.
There is up to 14 substitutes.
A substitute can be made
anytime except if they are
in the penalty. What I
don't know is for how
long?
The hockey players play
three 20 minute periods.
Sometimes I play three
20 minute periods.
The face-off circle is
for starting the game over
again, just in case somebody

not know or understand ("What I don't know is for how long?" and "I didn't know there was a face-off circle.").

The writer closes his piece by saying, "I will try to learn as much as I can about hockey."

The writer uses vocabulary specifically related to the topic (such as "referee," "face-off circle," and "penalty"), but he does not define these special terms.

The writer employs a straightforward tone.

Score Point 2 *continued*

falls. The circle they use
is the one they are close
to. I didn't know there
was a face-off circle. When
I play and someone falls
down we continue unless
they get hurt.
Every game refereed. My
question to this is why
are all the games refereed?
I always see a referee. If
they need to throw in
the puck why can't
a goalie do that.
Hockey is one of my
favorite sports. I will try

to learn as much as I can
about hockey.

Assessment Summary: "Rules of Hockey"

ELEMENTS		
	Needs Instruction	**Commentary**
Orientation and Context	• Introduces the topic. • Attempts to engage the reader. • May establish a context.	The writer introduces and attempts to engage the reader's interest by asserting that hockey is unique ("Hockey is the fastest team sport in the world."). He relates his personal experience as a hockey player, saying, "I started playing hockey when I was 8 years old." Instead of establishing a knowledgeable stance, the writer frequently comments on what he does not know or understand ("What I don't know is for how long?" and "I didn't know there was a face-off circle.").
Organization of Information	• Conveys a perspective. • Clusters details in an organizing structure.	The writer's perspective on the subject is that hockey "is the fastest team sport" and "a fun game too." Facts and details are loosely clustered around topics.
Development and Specificity of Information	• Develops information and reports on a topic, but may lack adequate and specific facts and information pertinent to the topic.	The writer develops information about the topic by explaining various rules, such as how many players play on each side, how many substitutes can be made, how long they play, the procedure for starting the game, how the games are refereed, etc. Facts and details are loosely clustered around these topics ("The hockey players play for three 20 minute periods. Sometimes I play three 20 minute periods."), but the writer does not describe the game itself.
Closure	• Typically provides a conclusion or concluding statement.	The writer closes his piece by saying, "I will try to learn as much as I can about hockey."
STRATEGIES		
	Needs Instruction	**Commentary**
Names and Vocabulary	• Uses names and specialized vocabulary related to the topic.	The writer uses vocabulary specifically related to the topic (such as "referee," "face-off circle," and "penalty"), but he does not define these special terms.
Other	• May include illustrations or graphics to support the text. • Employs a straightforward tone.	The writer employs a straightforward tone.
Note: The commentary highlights the elements and strategies in the student paper, focusing on how well the paper addresses the totality of the elements and strategies rather than on whether each is included.		

Next Steps in Instruction

The writer will benefit from instruction on gathering information about the topic, including well-developed and specific facts and information in the paper, and reporting information in ways that meet the reader's needs by including all the information that might be necessary for a reader who is not familiar with the sport.

Score Point 1

Report of Information Student Work and Commentary: "DBZ"

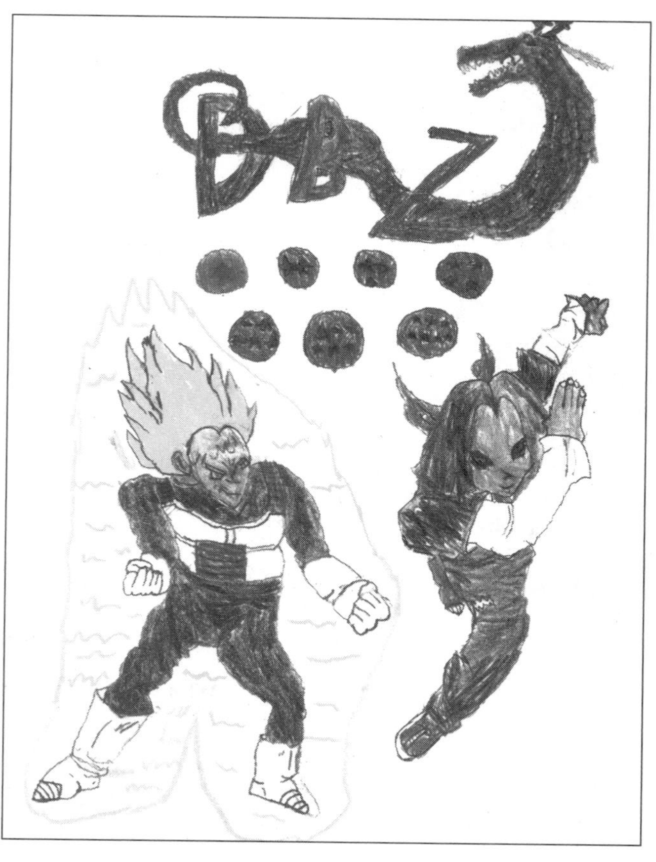

"DBZ" is written by a student who will need substantial instruction and support in order to produce work that meets the standard. The paper is problematic in several ways. First, the information is not always grouped appropriately; second, the writer does not make an effort to build the reader's understanding (for example, some terminology is very esoteric); and finally, the information provided is scant.

The writer introduces the topic of the piece in an answer to the first question-and-answer section of the text ("What is Dragon Ball Z?" Answer: "Dragon Ball Z is an animated television show...about competing and fighting.").

The organizational structure is a question-and-answer format; however, the information is frequently not grouped appropriately ("Some of the characters have powers, others don't" and "Z fighters are guys with super powers" appear in the section titled "What is Dragon Ball Z?"). Furthermore, comments about the characters' "attacks" appear in this section as well as the next one, titled "Who are the characters?"

The piece lacks adequate and specific information. For instance, the writer asks, "Who are the characters?" In response, he answers that there are many different characters, but he names only one: "Goku." He also describes the characters' powers in a very general way ("Their attacks come form the energy in their minds.").

In the conclusion, the reader is instructed to watch the show or log on to a website.

The writer uses some names associated with the topic ("Goku" and "Kamama") and provides illustrations.

Although the tone is straightforward, the information provided is scant.

Score Point 1 *continued*

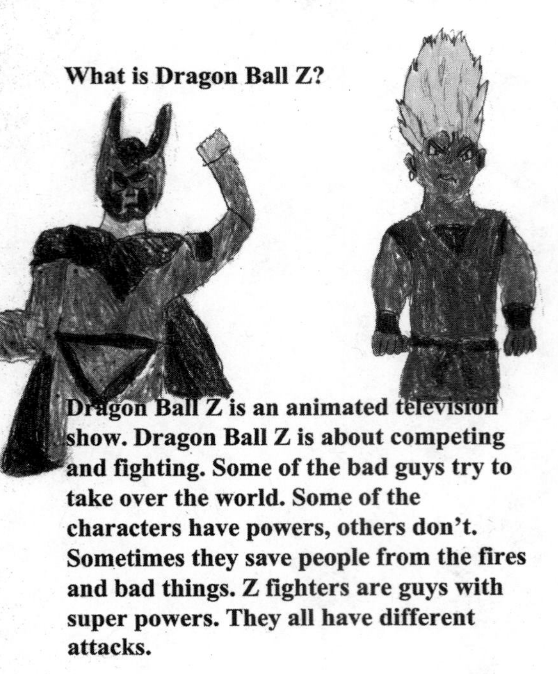

What is Dragon Ball Z?

Dragon Ball Z is an animated television show. Dragon Ball Z is about competing and fighting. Some of the bad guys try to take over the world. Some of the characters have powers, others don't. Sometimes they save people from the fires and bad things. Z fighters are guys with super powers. They all have different attacks.

Who are the characters?

There are lots of different characters and they like to fight. Some of them, like Goku are dead. They sometimes come back for a visit to see how everyone is doing. Goku like others have attacks like Spirit Ball and lots of other attacks. His trusted attack is the Kamama attack. Their attacks come form the energy in their minds.

Score Point 1 *continued*

How did they make the characters?

First they come up with a character from their imagination like Goku, my favorite character. They begin illustrating what comes to mind The producer soon had a cool cartoon show to play on television

Why did they make DB Z?

Dragon Ball and Dragon ball Z were made to entertain people who like action super heros and entertainment. It is a great show. I hope you like my book. To learn more about Dragon Ball Z. Watch the show or log on. to: www.dragonballz.com

Score Point 1 *continued*

Assessment Summary: "DBZ"

ELEMENTS		
	Needs Substantial Support	**Commentary**
Orientation and Context	• Introduces the topic. • May attempt to engage the reader. • Typically does not establish a context.	The writer introduces the topic of the piece in an answer to the first question-and-answer section of the text ("What is Dragon Ball Z?" Answer: "Dragon Ball Z is an animated television show...about competing and fighting.").
Organization of Information	• May create a simple list or use a loose organizational structure.	The organizational structure is a question-and-answer format; however, the information is frequently not grouped appropriately ("Some of the characters have powers, others don't" and "Z fighters are guys with super powers" appear in the section titled "What is Dragon Ball Z?"). Comments about the characters' "attacks" appear in this section as well as the next one, titled "Who are the characters?"
Development and Specificity of Information	• Develops information and reports on a topic, but typically lacks adequate and specific facts and information pertinent to the topic.	The piece lacks adequate and specific information. For instance, the writer asks, "Who are the characters?" In response, he answers that there are many different characters, but he names only one: "Goku." He also describes the characters' powers in a very general way ("Their attacks come form the energy in their minds.").
Closure	• Typically provides a conclusion or concluding statement.	In the conclusion, the reader is instructed to watch the show or log on to a website.

STRATEGIES		
	Needs Substantial Support	**Commentary**
Names and Vocabulary	• May use names and specialized vocabulary related to the topic.	The writer uses some names associated with the topic ("Goku" and "Kamama").
Other	• May include illustrations or graphics to support the text. • Employs a straightforward tone.	The writer uses illustrations to support the text. Although the tone is straightforward, the information provided is scant.
Note: The commentary highlights the elements and strategies in the student paper, focusing on how well the paper addresses the totality of the elements and strategies rather than on whether each is included.		

Roadmap for Development

The writer needs help with organization and with providing adequate information for a reader who may be unfamiliar with the topic. Organization is frequently problematic in informational pieces because clustering ideas is difficult. Perhaps some work with graphic organizers would help in this regard. The second problem, the inadequacy of information, can be addressed by having the writer work with response partners who may alert him to their need for additional information to clarify their understanding.

Instructions

Instructions (sometimes called procedures, functional writing, or process essays) tell readers how to do something or describe how something is done through a sequence of actions. Beverly Derewianka (1990) explains that this genre is very important in our society because it makes it possible for us to get things done. There are many subgenres of this kind of writing: appliance manuals, science experiments, craft instructions, recipes, directions to reach a destination or to build a model, game rules, etc. In school, this type of writing appears frequently in science, homemaking, art, and other classes that focus on processes as opposed to things.

Instructions are like narratives because they are basically chronological in structure; however, instructions describe steps in a process instead of events in time. Because they are chronological in structure, children who write narratives can easily learn how to organize this genre. Young writers usually have little, if any, difficulty sequencing the steps in a plan of action.

Instructions require students to have expertise they can draw on. Fortunately, students have much expertise, even at the primary level. They know how to play games, care for pets, carve pumpkins, make peanut butter sandwiches, and so on. Having something to write about is not a problem for children who write this genre. However, the degree of specificity required sometimes makes writing instructions difficult, as does the problem of engaging the reader. Very young writers will sometimes adopt a narrative stance, presenting steps as actions they take or have taken ("I plant a sed [seed]. I water my sed [seed]. I wat far a rot [waited for a root]."). But when students see good examples of instructions, and model their own text on the examples, they are less likely to simply recount. Some topics are simply much more difficult for young writers than others. Topics that are too broad or detailed (for instance, how to play soccer, how to build a model car) are often too difficult for students, especially for those whose writing generally does not meet the standard.

Orientation and Context

There is no single way to begin instructions, but at the very least, writers must identify the activity or process and the goal. Writers of this genre also provide context, both in the beginning and throughout the text. They may explain why actions are necessary or why steps have to be taken in a particular order. They may include comments on the significance, usefulness, entertainment value, or danger of the activity in order to engage the reader. Typically, young writers of this genre also establish their credentials. That is, they create a knowledgeable stance. In texts by adult writers of this genre, a knowledgeable stance is often assumed. In the case of young writers, pictures may play a large role in providing both context and essential information.

Organization and Development of Instructions

Like narratives, instructions are organized by time. But instead of events, steps in a process or activity are the deep structure for organization. The text is organized by a sequence of actions. Typically, writers begin with the first step in the process and proceed in time until the last step. Goals are identified, materials are listed, typically in order of use, and steps oriented toward achieving the goal are described.

Writers elaborate on and organize steps in the process in a variety of ways (for example, by providing diagrams, giving reasons for actions, and creating visual imagery through words and illustrations). They create expectations through the use of predictable structures. Headings, subheadings, numbers, etc. are often used to make the process easy to understand and follow. Because instructions are organized by steps in time, common linking words are used (before, during, after, first of all, finally, next, later, simultaneously, subsequently, immediately following, in the meantime). Writers also use transition phrases to make their instructions clear and easy to follow ("When you're all done with that..."). The reader is typically referred to in a general way (one/you), but sometimes the reader is not mentioned at all if the writer uses commands to signal the steps to take ("Take the top off the hamster cage.").

When writing in this genre, successful writers provide a specific guide to action (or a specific description of the activity). They describe the steps or key components in detail, anticipating a reader's need for information and foreseeing likely points of confusion. They explain what to do, and how and why to do it ("Always try to give your hamster food at the same time each day. Then they can learn how to get up at the same time each day."). Sometimes they comment on who would need to know how to do the activity. They explain precautions that should be taken and warn about possible difficulties. They anticipate places where problems are likely to occur ("Food bowl heavy enough so the hamster can't pick it up"; "Don't give them citrus fruits, Onions, or garlic.").

Effective writers of this genre provide specific details (to explain how, what, where, and when), and they adjust the level of detail to fit the goal. They use diagrams or illustrations as complements and to supplement the verbal information in the text. They describe materials, tools, and preparations needed to carry out the process, providing precise information about size, length, weight, number, types, and so on. They define technical terms and explain steps in the process.

Closure

Often the last step of the process is the conclusion of the writing. Although instructions may not always have a formal conclusion, writers typically provide some sort of closure. Sometimes writers explain the significance of the process or summarize the main steps. Young writers sometimes use a simple concluding statement to say how one could use the results if the process leads to a product ("Maybe if you make enough you can sell them to people..."). Sometimes they simply exhort the reader to engage in the activity ("Now that you know something about Wakeboarding, get out their and wakeboard!").

Instructions in Fifth Grade 

At this age, many students have a good understanding of the instructions genre and a variety of strategies for dealing with it. Less able writers, however, may still be struggling with the challenges the genre presents. They may simply announce the topic. They may not organize appropriately the steps to be followed, and the steps they provide may be too general to enable a reader to follow them. Their writing may lack coherence and detail, making it difficult for the reader to know what to do. Frequently, they fail to anticipate the reader's need for information. For example, one young writer advised readers to "First serv the hackysack to one of the people that your playing with. That person should hit the hackysack 3 or more times then cach it..." but he failed to inform the reader that hacky sack players both serve and hit with their feet. Nearly all writers at this grade level provide closure to their writing, even the less able ones who do not meet the standard. A common strategy is to encourage the reader to engage in the activity.

Writers who meet the standard at fifth grade introduce the topic, engage the reader, and establish a context ("If you have a hamster and don't now how to take care of it you should read this book. It tells all about them."). They convey a knowledgeable stance. They provide a specific guide to action, describing the steps or key components of the task in detail. They anticipate possible problems and explain how to deal with them ("Food bowl heavy enough so the hamster can't pick it up"; "Never ever hit your hamster or it will want revenge and it will bite you."). They explain why steps have to be taken in a particular order ("Always try to give your hamster food at the same time each day. Then they can learn how to get up at the same time each day."). Their instructions may be organized into sections, but within each section, steps are ordered by time. For instance, a section on cleaning cages in a piece about hamsters begins with the first step to take ("Take off the top of the hamster cage."). They provide closure. These writers also use language that is straightforward and clear. They employ a variety of transition devices, including simple words and phrases ("First," "After that"), but they also use clauses within more complex syntactical structures that make it easy for the reader to follow the steps ("When you are all done with that..."; "After you wash and rinse it...").

Instructions Rubrics Elements

	5 Exceeds Standard*	4 Meets Standard
Orientation and Context	• Introduces the topic. • Establishes a context. • Engages the reader. • Conveys a knowledgeable stance.	• Introduces the topic. • Establishes a context. • Engages the reader. • Conveys a knowledgeable stance.
Organization and Development of Instructions	• Provides a specific guide to action with steps that are appropriately sequenced and comprehensive. • Describes the steps or key components in detail. • Provides specific details to help the reader understand the instructions (e.g., "Use a soap that does not have a strong smell…"). • Elaborates on actions (e.g., by providing reasons for actions or explaining why actions have to be taken in a particular order). • Anticipates a reader's need for information.	• Provides a specific guide to action with steps that are appropriately sequenced and comprehensive. • Describes the steps or key components in detail. • Provides specific details to help the reader understand the instructions (e.g., "Use a soap that does not have a strong smell…"). • Elaborates on actions (e.g., by providing reasons for actions or explaining why actions have to be taken in a particular order). • Anticipates a reader's need for information.
Closure	• Provides closure.	• Provides closure.

	3 Needs Revision	2 Needs Instruction	1 Needs Substantial Support
Orientation and Context	• Introduces the topic. • Establishes a context. • Engages the reader. • Conveys a knowledgeable stance.	• May announce the topic. • Attempts to establish a context. • Attempts to engage the reader.	• May announce the topic only with the title. • May attempt to establish a context. • May attempt to engage the reader.
Organization and Development of Instructions	• Provides a general series of steps or actions. • Organizes steps sequentially. • Provides details to help the reader understand the instructions. • May elaborate on actions (e.g., by providing reasons for actions or explaining why actions have to be taken in a particular order). • May anticipate a reader's need for information.	• Provides a very general series of steps or actions (readers may have to infer some of the steps). • May not organize steps or actions sequentially. • Provides some details to help the reader understand the instructions. • Provides little or no elaboration on actions. • May not anticipate a reader's need for information.	• Provides a very general series of steps (readers may have to infer some of the steps). • May not organize the steps or actions sequentially. • Provides few details to help the reader understand the instructions. • Provides little or no elaboration on actions. • Typically does not anticipate a reader's need for information.
Closure	• Provides closure.	• Provides closure.	• Provides closure.

*The criteria that define score points 5 and 4 are identical. This is intentional. What distinguishes a 5 from a 4 is not the presence or absence of a particular element or strategy. Rather, it is the overall quality of execution and the level of language the writer employs. Writers of score point 5 papers bring something to the text that may not be provided by instruction—a deep understanding or passion for the topic and the genre.

Instructions Rubrics Strategies

	5 Exceeds Standard*	4 Meets Standard
Transition Devices	• Uses a variety of transition words, phrases, and clauses to indicate sequence of steps (e.g., first, third, during, before, "When you play with your bird…"). • May use formatting to highlight specific categories of information or to signal transitions between steps.	• Uses a variety of transition words, phrases, and clauses to indicate sequence of steps (e.g., first, third, during, before, "When you play with your bird…"). • May use formatting to highlight specific categories of information or to signal transitions between steps.
Other	• May use drawings or graphics to illustrate the instructions.	• May use drawings or graphics to illustrate the instructions.

	3 Needs Revision	2 Needs Instruction	1 Needs Substantial Support
Transition Devices	• May use some simple transition words (e.g., first, now, then) or number the steps. • May use formatting to highlight specific categories of information or to signal transitions between steps.	• May use some simple transition words (e.g., first, now, then) or number the steps. • May attempt to use formatting to highlight specific categories of information or to signal transitions between steps.	• May use some simple transition words (e.g., first, now, then) or number the steps. • May attempt to use formatting to highlight specific categories of information or to signal transitions between steps.
Other	• May use drawings or graphics to illustrate the instructions.	• May use drawings or graphics to illustrate the instructions.	• May use drawings or graphics to illustrate the instructions.

*The criteria that define score points 5 and 4 are identical. This is intentional. What distinguishes a 5 from a 4 is not the presence or absence of a particular element or strategy. Rather, it is the overall quality of execution and the level of language the writer employs. Writers of score point 5 papers bring something to the text that may not be provided by instruction—a deep understanding or passion for the topic and the genre.

Score Point 5

Instructions Student Work and Commentary: "How to Take Care of a Hamster"

In "How to Take Care of a Hamster," the student demonstrates her expertise about hamsters through her specific instructions about hamster care. The piece also includes substantial evidence of the author's craft, including the writer's use of specific detail, graphic organizers, and humor. The author's confident tone and specific details combine to make this an informative and lively piece of writing. This carefully organized and illustrated piece exceeds the standard for writing instructions in fifth grade.

The introduction states the topic and engages the reader by explaining why the piece is useful ("If you have a hamster and don't know how to take care of it you should read this book.").

The "Dedication" page establishes a context and creates a knowledgeable stance by informing readers that the student owns two hamsters ("I dedicat my story to my hamsters Maryjane and Bluecheese.").

The table of contents outlines the organizing structure of the piece by listing important aspects of

Score Point 5 *continued*

Table of Contents

hamster care ("Needs of the Hamster," "Feeding," "Cleaning," and "Training"). The table of contents also directs the reader to the appropriate page.

Within each chapter, the author provides steps in order by time (the first task for cleaning is "Take the top off the hamster cage."). The drawings in each section help clarify her instructions.

The writer also provides specific guides to action ("Always try to give your hamster food at the same time each day. Then they can learn how to get up at the same time each day.").

In "Feeding," the author lists a variety of foods for hamsters, and she gives detailed instructions for feeding ("Don't give them citrus fruits, Onions, or garlic.").

The writer anticipates and answers readers' potential questions about what type of supplies to buy by providing detailed descriptions of the needed supplies ("Food bowl heavy enough so the hamster can't pick it up.").

The writer provides closure on the last page with the sentence "I hope you liked this book. bye" and a picture of a waving hamster.

The piece includes transition phrases that make her instructions clear and easy to follow ("When you are all done with that…").

The illustrations of hamster equipment, drawings of hamsters from different angles, and humorous captions (one hamster asks, "Hay where are you taking me?") serve both to inform and engage the reader.

Score Point 5 *continued*

Dedication Page

I dedicat my story to my hamsters. Maryjane and Bluecheese. I wish that they can Knew how to read So they could read my book. But they can't so oh well...

Introduction.......

If you have a hamster and don't now how to take Care of it you should read this book. It tells all about them.

Needs of the Hamster

Of Course you will need.....
Water bottle one that is for a hamster
Food bowl heavy enough so the hamster can't pick it up
- Acage one so that the hamster can run around in
- Food hamster food is a dry food buy a full bag.
- Shedding for the botum of the cage.
- Toy always have a wheel and a toy. The wheel should be solid

Score Point 5 *continued*

Feeding Feeding Feeding Feeding

Only give your hamster one tablespone of food each day. Throw away the left overs the next day. Always try to give your hamster food at the same time each day. Then they can learn how to get up at the same time each day (well, what I do is, before I go to school I throw away the left overs and put in new food. You should do that too) Well at the the pet shop, there is an ialley that has food for your pet. They are labled hamster food, mice food, cabbaile food etc. but only get the hamster food and buy a full bag.

You can also buy, tomato, graps, carrots, watermelon, cucumber, white cabbage and

↓ Sunflower seeds unsailted

Food list

Sunflowerseeds unsailted
corn
Locust beans
maize
oats
penuts
rolled barley
Flaked pea

apples. You should give your hamster a little tiny bit only. Half a grap, thats how small. Dont give them citrus fruits. Onions, or Garlic. All the food you need is mostly at the pet shop. There in a bag but they are dry foods.

Cleaning is very easy. All you need to do is.......
Take the top off the hamster cage.
Take the food bowl, hamsters toys bedding out.

If there is water in the bowl take that out too.
Put your hamster in a safe place.

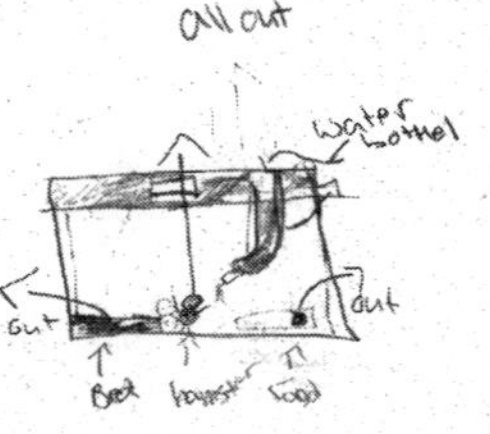

Score Point 5 *continued*

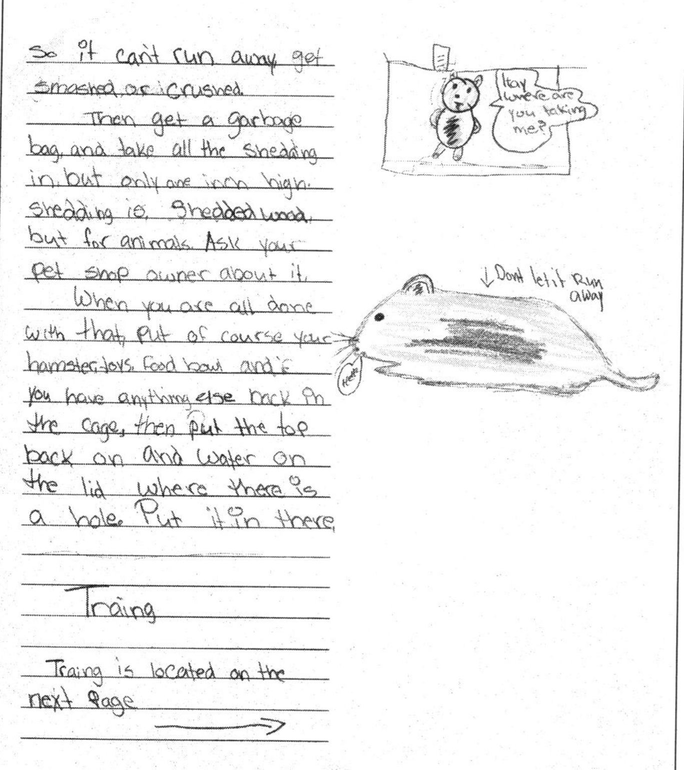

So it can't run away get smashed or crushed.

Then get a garbage bag and take all the shedding in but only one inch high. shedding is shedded wood but for animals. Ask your pet shop owner about it.

When you are all done with that put of course your hamster toys, food bowl and if you have anything else back in the cage, then put the top back on and water on the lid where there is a hole. Put it in there.

Traing

Traing is located on the next page →

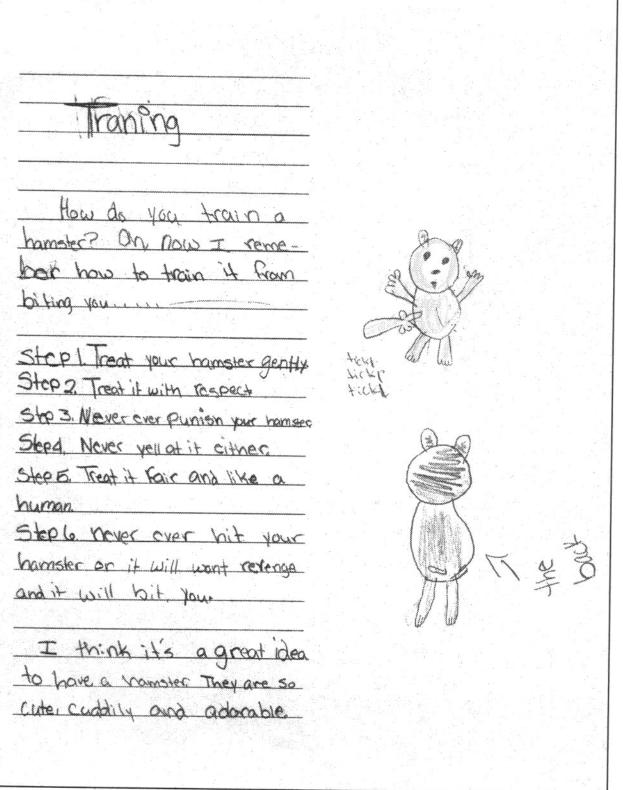

Traning

How do you train a hamster? Oh, now I remeber how to train it from biting you......

Step 1. Treat your hamster gently

Step 2. Treat it with respect

Step 3. Never ever punish your hamster

Step 4. Never yell at it either.

Step 5. Treat it fair and like a human

Step 6. Never ever hit your hamster or it will want revenge and it will bit you.

I think it's a great idea to have a hamster. They are so cute, cuddily and adorable.

Score Point 5 *continued*

I think everyone should have two hamsters. I hope you liked this book. bye.

bye bye

Assessment Summary: "How to Take Care of a Hamster"

ELEMENTS		
	Exceeds Standard	**Commentary**
Orientation and Context	• Introduces the topic. • Establishes a context. • Engages the reader. • Conveys a knowledgeable stance.	The introduction states the topic and engages the reader by explaining why the piece is useful ("If you have a hamster and don't know how to take care of it you should read this book."). The "Dedication" page establishes a context and creates a knowledgeable stance by informing readers that the student owns two hamsters ("I dedicat my story to my hamsters. Maryjane and Bluecheese.").
Organization and Development of Instructions	• Provides a specific guide to action with steps that are appropriately sequenced and comprehensive. • Describes the steps or key components in detail. • Provides specific details to help the reader understand the instructions (e.g., "Use a soap that does not have a strong smell…"). • Elaborates on actions (e.g., by providing reasons for actions or explaining why actions have to be taken in a particular order). • Anticipates a reader's need for information.	The table of contents outlines the organizing structure of the piece by listing important aspects of hamster care ("Needs of the Hamster," "Feeding," "Cleaning," and "Training"). The table of contents also directs the reader to the appropriate page. Within each chapter, the author provides steps in order by time (the first task for cleaning is "Take the top off the hamster cage."). The drawings in each section help clarify her instructions. The writer also provides specific guides to action ("Always try to give your hamster food at the same time each day. Then they can learn how to get up at the same time each day."). In "Feeding," the author lists a variety of foods for hamsters, and she gives detailed instructions for feeding ("Don't give them citrus fruits, Onions, or garlic."). The writer anticipates and answers readers' potential questions about what type of supplies to buy by providing detailed descriptions of the needed supplies ("Food bowl heavy enough so the hamster can't pick it up.").
Closure	• Provides closure.	The writer provides closure on the last page (the sentence "I hope you liked this book. bye" and a picture of a waving hamster).

STRATEGIES		
	Exceeds Standard	**Commentary**
Transition Devices	• Uses a variety of transition words, phrases, and clauses to indicate sequence of steps (e.g., first, third, during, before, "When you play with your bird..."). • May use formatting to highlight specific categories of information or to signal transitions between steps.	The piece includes transition phrases that make her instructions clear and easy to follow ("When you are all done with that...").
Other	• May use drawings or graphics to illustrate the instructions.	The illustrations of hamster equipment, drawings of hamsters from different angles, and humorous captions (one hamster asks, "Hay where are you taking me?") serve both to inform and engage the reader.
Note: The commentary highlights the elements and strategies in the student paper, focusing on how well the paper addresses the totality of the elements and strategies rather than on whether each is included.		

Score Point 4

Instructions Student Work and Commentary: "How to do a Mountain Goat Clogging Combination"

How to do a Mountain Goat Clogging Combination

People think that clogging is a dance from Sweden with people stomping around in big wooden shoes. That might have been true a long time ago, but hey we're in the 21st century and we're clogging in style. One of my favorite steps is the Mountain Goat combination. Don't worry about shoes, you can clogg with out them. Have fun!

"Double step, double slide"

First you need to do a double step with your left foot. To do this (see figure 1) scuff the ball of your left foot up. Then scuff it back behind you (see figure 2) with the ball of your left foot. Then step down.

After that scuff your right foot up in front of you and behind you again, barely of to the side and bent (see figure 3). Then you hop on your left foot (see figure 4), right leg still in the air.

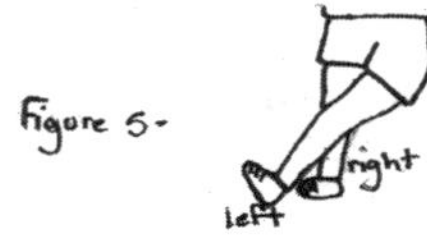

Bring your right foot behind your left foot and shift your weight to your right foot and tap your left heel on the ground (see figure 5) and step on your left foot in step of your right.

Figure 5-
right
left

"How to do a Mountain Goat Clogging Combination" carefully guides readers through the steps of a complicated dance combination. This carefully illustrated piece meets the standard for writing instructions at fifth grade.

The writer establishes a context and creates a knowledgeable stance by anticipating readers' uninformed assumptions about clogging ("People think that clogging is a dance from Sweden with people stomping around in big wooden shoes.").

She engages readers by challenging them to update their thinking about clogging ("hey we're in the 21st century and we're clogging in style.") and by encouraging them to "Have fun!"

The piece provides a specific guide to action by breaking the Mountain Goat Clogging combination into a series of shorter steps, including the "Double step, double slide," "Fancy double," and "Clap, Ball Heel." She provides readers with specific tips about clogging technique ("Caution: Make sure that the sounds of the balls and heels are separate."), and her use of specialized clogging vocabulary demonstrates her expertise to readers.

The descriptions of each step are accompanied by illustrations that play an important role in explaining the steps to readers. Each step is described in detail, and the drawings provide graphic illustrations that elaborate on her written instructions. The illustrations,

Score Point 4 *continued*

Next step on the ball of your right foot and scuff the heel of your left foot up and bend it in front of you so it;s almost flat enough to balance a coke can, (see figure 6) and hop on your right leg.

Figure 6- left left right

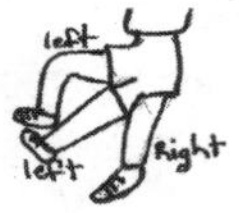

"Fancy double"

To do a fancy double you do two double steps by (see figure 1) scuffing the ball of your left foot up in front of you and then again behind you and step on your left foot.

Now lean back on your left leg (which is behind your right) and tap the heel of your right foot on the ground and step on your right foot. Do this two times. (see figure 7)

Figure 7- right left

"Mountain Goat"

Now you do the Mountain Goat. (see figure 1) Do a double step on your left foot. Then cross your right foot over your left and step on the ball of you right foot and shift your weight to your right foot. Next tap the toe of your left foot on the ground behind your right foot and step on the ball of your left foot still behind your right. Then you take your right foot and step on the ball of it so it's beside your left and and tap the heel of your left in the front and step on your left foot. Then bring your right foot and step step near the back of your left foot. Next flap the heel of your left foot up in front and hop on our right foot left leg still in the air able to balance a can.

labeled as "Figures," clarify the instructions for readers ("Then you hop on your left foot (see figure 4), right leg still in the air."). Her careful integration of pictures and written instructions provide specific details for readers.

After introducing the "Double step, Double slide" and the "Fancy double," the writer begins to lead readers through the Mountain Goat clogging combination ("Now you do the Mountain Goat."). At this point, the sentences become longer and the directions are more difficult to follow ("Then cross your right foot over your left and step on the ball of you right foot and shift your weight to your right foot."). The writer aids comprehension by referring to the figures and by using clogging terms that she has previously introduced and explained ("Do a double step on your left foot.").

The writer anticipates readers' needs by telling them they do not need special shoes for clogging.

The writer provides closure by encouraging readers to try the Mountain Goat combination again ("practice makes perfect, so don't get upset if you didn't make it the first time.").

The piece includes transition words to clarify the instructions ("First," "After that"). The writer uses short sentences to describe the "Double step, Double slide" and the "Fancy double," but the sentences need to be short so that the reader is not confused.

Score Point 4 *continued*

"Clap, Ball, Heel"

Since your left foot is open clap and step on the ball of your left foot shifting your weight to your left foot, and tap your right heel in front of your left and step on the ball of your right foot shifting your weight to your right foot and tap your left heel on the ground in front of your right foot and step on the ball of your left foot. Then clap and do the same only starting with your right foot.

CAUTION:Make sure that the sounds of the balls and heels are separate.

Fun wasn't it. Thanks for giving it a go! Remember practice makes perfect, so don't get upset if you didn't get it the first time.

Score Point 4 *continued*

Assessment Summary: "How to do a Mountain Goat Clogging Combination"

ELEMENTS		
	Meets Standard	**Commentary**
Orientation and Context	• Introduces the topic. • Establishes a context. • Engages the reader. • Conveys a knowledgeable stance.	The writer establishes a context and creates a knowledgeable stance by anticipating readers' uninformed assumptions about clogging ("People think that clogging is a dance from Sweden with people stomping around in big wooden shoes."). She engages readers by challenging them to update their thinking about clogging ("hey we're in the 21st century and we're clogging in style.") and by encouraging them to "Have fun!"
Organization and Development of Instructions	• Provides a specific guide to action with steps that are appropriately sequenced and comprehensive. • Describes the steps or key components in detail. • Provides specific details to help the reader understand the instructions (e.g., "Use a soap that does not have a strong smell..."). • Elaborates on actions (e.g., by providing reasons for actions or explaining why actions have to be taken in a particular order). • Anticipates a reader's need for information.	The piece provides a specific guide to action by breaking the Mountain Goat Clogging combination into a series of shorter steps, including the "Double step, double slide," "Fancy double," and "Clap, Ball Heel." She provides readers with specific tips about clogging technique ("Caution: Make sure that the sounds of the balls and heels are separate."), and her use of specialized clogging vocabulary demonstrates her expertise to readers. The descriptions of each step are accompanied by illustrations that play an important role in explaining the steps to readers. Each step is described in detail, and the drawings provide graphic illustrations that elaborate on her written instructions. The illustrations, labeled as "Figures," clarify the instructions for readers ("Then you hop on your left foot (see figure 4), right leg still in the air."). Her careful integration of pictures and written instructions provide specific details for readers. After introducing the "Double step, Double slide" and the "Fancy double," the writer begins to lead readers through the Mountain Goat clogging combination ("Now you do the Mountain Goat."). At this point, the sentences become longer and the directions are more difficult to follow ("Then cross your right foot over your left and step on the ball of you right foot and shift your weight to your right foot."). The writer aids comprehension by referring to the figures and by using clogging terms that she has previously introduced and explained ("Do a double step on your left foot."). The writer anticipates readers' needs by telling them they do not need special shoes for clogging.
Closure	• Provides closure.	The writer provides closure by encouraging readers to try the Mountain Goat combination again ("practice makes perfect, so don't get upset if you didn't make it the first time.").

STRATEGIES		
	Meets Standard	**Commentary**
Transition Devices	• Uses a variety of transition words, phrases, and clauses to indicate sequence of steps (e.g., first, third, during, before, "When you play with your bird…"). • May use formatting to highlight specific categories of information or to signal transitions between steps.	The piece includes transition words to clarify the instructions ("First," "After that"). The writer uses short sentences to describe the "Double step, Double slide" and the "Fancy double," but the sentences need to be short so that the reader is not confused.
Other	• May use drawings or graphics to illustrate the instructions.	The illustrations, labeled as "Figures," clarify the instructions for readers ("Then you hop on your left foot (see figure 4), right leg still in the air.").
Note: The commentary highlights the elements and strategies in the student paper, focusing on how well the paper addresses the totality of the elements and strategies rather than on whether each is included.		

Score Point 3

Instructions Student Work and Commentary: "How to Clean your ROOM!"

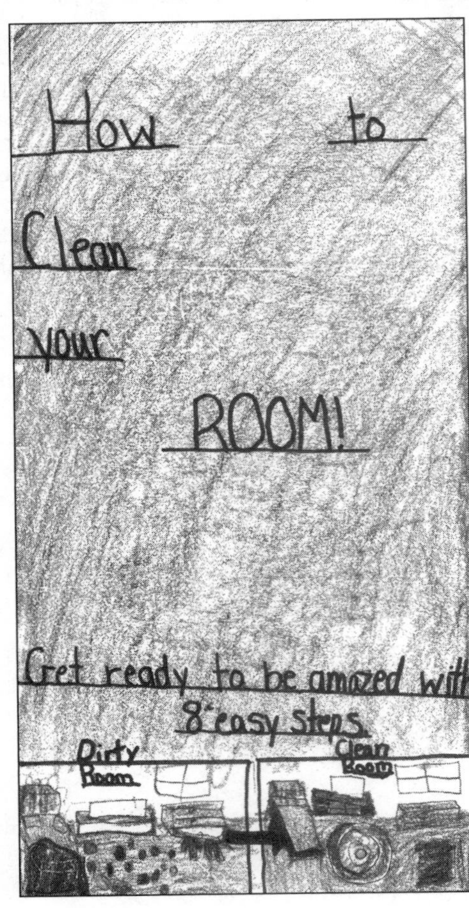

Want to learn how to clean your room. No, No, not shoving it all under your bed. The real way OK then read this pamphlet.

Section one: When is your room dirty?

Your room is dirty when:

1. There are clothes on the floor.
2. When you can't get to your bed without stubbing your toe.
3. When the bed isn't made.
4. When all your toys or things are on your floor.

Now that you know the symptoms give your dirty room the medicine.

Patterned after an informational pamphlet, "How to Clean your ROOM!" explains how to determine when a room is dirty and provides readers with instructions for cleaning a dirty room. The piece approaches but does not meet the standard for writing instructions in fifth grade.

The writer engages readers with the subheading "Get ready to be amazed with 8 easy steps." The writer also uses humor to engage his readers ("No, No, not shoving it all under your bed").

The writer establishes a context for the piece and conveys a knowledgeable stance by explaining that he will teach readers to clean their rooms the "real way," rather than "shoving it all under your bed," the implication being that he is experienced in both routes.

The piece is divided into two topics that are organized by time: "When is your room dirty?" and "The Saturday clean." Section one outlines the problem by giving readers a list to help them determine if their rooms are dirty ("When you can't get to bed without stubbing your toe."). Section two proposes a series of general steps to solve the problem of a dirty room. The writer describes "Section one" as a group of "symptoms" and "Section two" as the "medicine" needed to treat those symptoms.

The writer's instructions often lack specific details ("make your bed by pulling up the covers to the top

Score Point 3 *continued*

Section two: The Saturday clean.

This will take about 20-30 minutes every Saturday or weekend.

The things that you will need:

1. Your hands maybe gloves
2. 2 Big black garbage bags

1. First pick up all the blankets on the floor or on your bed and make your bed by pulling up the covers to the top of the bed.

2. Pick up all the clothes on the floor and put them in a clothes hamper or clothes pile.

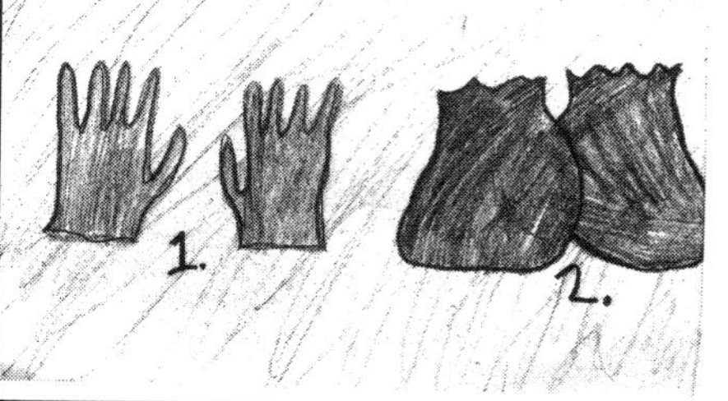

3. Take a big black plastic bag and put all the toys or things that you want in the bag and put it in the closet.
4. Take another big black bag and put all the garbage in it and put that bag in the garbage.
5. Then if there is anything that you want left on the floor put it in the toys or thing bag.
6. Last grab the vacuum and vacuum the floor.

Now you REALLY know how to clean your room and when people come over they "Ahh" it.

of the bed."). Also, the cleaning process he describes is not so different from the technique of "shoving it all under your bed" ("Take a big black plastic bag and put all the toys or things that you want in the bag and put it in the closet.").

The writer attempts to anticipate readers' needs by providing a list of supplies, but the list includes only two items. The supply list does not include a vacuum cleaner, despite the fact that the writer describes vacuuming as the final step in the cleaning process.

The final statement provides closure and reveals the writer's sense of humor ("Now you REALLY know how to clean your room and when people come over they 'Ahh' it.").

The steps for cleaning a room are numbered, and the writer includes transition words (such as "First," "Then," "Last") to guide the reader through the cleaning process.

A drawing of a medicine bottle with the label "Clean Room Medicine" illustrates the metaphor for readers.

Assessment Summary: "How to Clean your ROOM!"

ELEMENTS		
	Needs Revision	**Commentary**
Orientation and Context	• Introduces the topic. • Establishes a context. • Engages the reader. • Conveys a knowledgeable stance.	The writer engages readers with the subheading "Get ready to be amazed with 8 easy steps." The writer also uses humor to engage his readers ("No, No, not shoving it all under your bed"). The writer establishes a context for the piece and conveys a knowledgeable stance by explaining that he will teach readers to clean their rooms the "real way," rather than "shoving it all under your bed," the implication being that he is experienced in both routes.
Organization and Development of Instructions	• Provides a general series of steps or actions. • Organizes steps sequentially. • Provides details to help the reader understand the instructions. • May elaborate on actions (e.g., by providing reasons for actions or explaining why actions have to be taken in a particular order). • May anticipate a reader's need for information.	The piece is divided into two topics that are organized by time: "When is your room dirty?" and "The Saturday clean." Section one outlines the problem by giving readers a list to help them determine if their rooms are dirty ("When you can't get to bed without stubbing your toe."). Section two proposes a series of general steps to solve the problem of a dirty room. The writer describes "Section one" as a group of "symptoms" and "Section two" as the "medicine" needed to treat those symptoms. The writer's instructions often lack specific details ("make your bed by pulling up the covers to the top of the bed."). Also, the cleaning process he describes is not so different from the technique of "shoving it all under your bed" ("Take a big black plastic bag and put all the toys or things that you want in the bag and put it in the closet."). The writer attempts to anticipate readers' needs by providing a list of supplies, but the list includes only two items. The supply list does not include a vacuum cleaner, despite the fact that the writer describes vacuuming as the final step in the cleaning process.
Closure	• Provides closure.	The final statement provides closure and reveals the writer's sense of humor ("Now you REALLY know how to clean your room and when people come over they 'Ahh' it.").

STRATEGIES		
	Needs Revision	**Commentary**
Transition Devices	• Uses transition words to indicate sequence of steps (e.g., first, third, during, before, then). • May use formatting to highlight specific categories of information or to signal transitions between steps.	The steps for cleaning a room are numbered, and the writer includes transition words (such as "First," "Then," "Last") to guide the reader through the cleaning process.
Other	• May use drawings or graphics to illustrate the instructions.	A drawing of a medicine bottle with the label "Clean Room Medicine" illustrates the metaphor for readers.
Note: The commentary highlights the elements and strategies in the student paper, focusing on how well the paper addresses the totality of the elements and strategies rather than on whether each is included.		

Possible Conference Topics

The writer will benefit from a conference to discuss imagining, and describing, all the possible ways a child's room could be dirty, as well as all the possible supplies needed for cleaning the room, and using details to elaborate on depictions of "usual" behaviors.

Score Point 2

Instructions Student Work and Commentary: "How to play different game's with a hackysack"

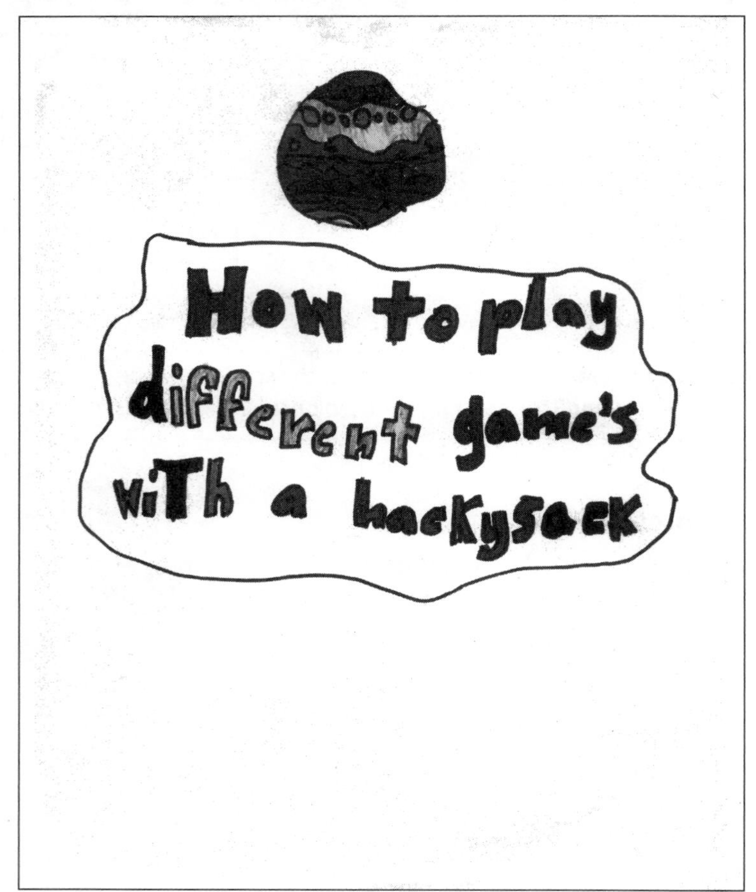

"How to play different game's with a hackysack" reveals a writer who needs instruction in order to be able to meet the standard for writing instructions in fifth grade. In this piece, the writer demonstrates familiarity with many of the conventions of this genre, but his explanations of hacky sack games often lack details, making it difficult for the reader to know what to do.

The writer attempts to engage the reader in the introduction by introducing the topic ("All you need for this game is a hackysack, some friends and a wide open space and I'll teach you.").

The piece is organized into four sections—three games and a glossary. The table of contents outlines the organization of the piece, but it does not specifically name the games the writer will discuss ("Game One" and "Game Two").

In each game, the writer presents a series of steps for readers, but the lack of specific details often makes it difficult for the reader to know what to do. For instance, the writer tells readers, "First serv the hackysack to one of the people that your playing with. That person should hit the hackysack 3 or more times then cach it..." but he does not provide details about *how* to serve or hit a hacky sack. A reader with a general knowledge of the sport would understand that serving and hitting are done with the feet, but the writer does not explain that for readers. Instead, the reader must rely on previous knowledge of hacky sack

Score Point 2 *continued*

Table of contents

games to infer the writer's meaning. Also, the writer explains how participants "get a G" and "get an O," but he does not explain whether earning letters is good or bad or how a player wins.

The writer's discussion of game three, called "Throw it," is more specific ("First thing is get a cupel of frainds that want to play. and after you do that find a big space like a football field."). He explains how the teams accumulate points ("if that team that trys to cach it missies it your team get's a point, but if they cach it, you don't get a point."), but he does not specify how a team wins.

The "glossary" attempts to provide specific details about the sport by defining terms for readers who may be unfamiliar with hacky sack play. The writer's definition of a hacky sack provides new information for unfamiliar readers. Like the writer's discussion of the games, however, some definitions are too general to be useful. For instance, the definition of "keepup" does not mention that players do not use their hands or arms when playing ("it's a game that involves keeping a hackysack in the air as long as you can without letting it hit the ground.").

The final sentence, "Do you got it?" provides closure to the instructions.

There is a clear transition between each game ("The secend game I am going to teach you is called keepup and this is how you play."), and the writer uses simple transition words ("First" and "But") to give the piece coherence.

Score Point 2 *continued*

Introduction→ All you need for this game is a hackysack, Some friends and a wide open space. and I'll teach you.

The first game that I am going to teach you is G.o.d. and this is how you play. First serv the hackysack to one of the people that your playing with. That person should hit the hackysack 3 or more times then cach it and throw the hackysack at eneyone your playing with, and if you hit them, they get a G. but if you miss, they don't get a letter. If they cach it when you throw it at them, they could throw it at you. and you get a G. But if they hit you agen you get an O. and so on.

The secend game I am going to teach you is called Keepup and this is how you play. First Serv the hackysack, into the air and hit it without useing your hand's or arm's. It's hard at first, but it gets more easyer when you practice. But try not to let the hack hackysack hit the ground or you will have to Start all over agen. So try this game and see how long you could keep it up.

Score Point 2 *continued*

Know the third game that I am going to teach you is called Throw it and this is how you play. First thing is get a cupel of frainds that want to play. and after you do that find a big space like a football fild. Make teams and then separate the teams on both sides of the fild. Throw the hackysack to the other team and they have to cach it. But if that team that trys to cach it missies it your team get's a point, but if they cach it, you dont get a point. Do you got it?

glossary

football field — is a 100 yard field where football is playd.

G.O.d – is a game that involves throwing a hackysack at someone.

Hackysack – is a nitted ball with beans inside.

Keepup – it's a game that involves keeping a hackysack in the air as long as you can without letting it hit the ground.

throw it – it's a game that involves throwing a hacky sack over a field.

Assessment Summary: "How to play different game's with a hackysack"

ELEMENTS		
	Needs Instruction	**Commentary**
Orientation and Context	• May announce the topic. • Attempts to establish a context. • Attempts to engage the reader.	The writer attempts to engage the reader in the introduction by introducing the topic ("All you need for this game is a hackysack, some friends and a wide open space and I'll teach you.").
Organization and Development of Instructions	• Provides a very general series of steps or actions (readers may have to infer some of the steps). • May not organize steps or actions sequentially. • Provides some details to help the reader understand the instructions. • Provides little or no elaboration on actions. • May not anticipate a reader's need for information.	The piece is organized into four sections—three games and a glossary. The Table of Contents outlines the organization of the piece, but it does not specifically name the games the writer will discuss ("Game One" and "Game Two"). In each game, the writer presents a series of steps for readers, but the lack of specific details often makes it difficult for the reader to know what to do. For instance, the writer tells readers, "First serv the hackysack to one of the people that your playing with. That person should hit the hackysack 3 or more times then cach it..." but he does not provide details about how to serve or hit a hacky sack. A reader with a general knowledge of the sport would understand that serving and hitting are done with the feet, but the writer does not explain that for readers. Instead, the reader must rely on previous knowledge of hacky sack games to infer the writer's meaning. Also, the writer explains how participants "get a G" and "get an O," but he does not explain whether earning letters is good or bad or how a player wins. The writer's discussion of game three, called "Throw it," is more specific ("First thing is get a cupel of frainds that want to play. and after you do that find a big space like a football field."). He explains how the teams accumulate points ("if that team that trys to cach it missies it your team get's a point, but if they cach it, you don't get a point."), but he does not specify how a team wins. The "glossary" attempts to provide specific details about the sport by defining terms for readers who may be unfamiliar with hacky sack play. The writer's definition of a hacky sack provides new information for unfamiliar readers. Like the writer's discussion of the games, however, some definitions are too general to be useful. For instance, the definition of "keepup" does not mention that players do not use their hands or arms when playing ("it's a game that involves keeping a hackysack in the air as long as you can without letting it hit the ground.").
Closure	• Provides closure.	The final sentence, "Do you got it?" provides closure to the instructions.

STRATEGIES		
	Needs Instruction	**Commentary**
Transition Devices	• May use some simple transition words (e.g., first, now, then) or number the steps. • May attempt to use formatting to highlight specific categories of information or to signal transitions between steps.	There is a clear transition between each game ("The secend game I am going to teach you is called keepup and this is how you play."), and the writer uses simple transition words ("First" and "But") to give the piece coherence.
Other	• May use drawings or graphics to illustrate the instructions.	
Note: The commentary highlights the elements and strategies in the student paper, focusing on how well the paper addresses the totality of the elements and strategies rather than on whether each is included.		

Next Steps in Instruction

This writer will benefit from instruction on describing a game or activity to someone who has never played it, anticipating and addressing a reader's need for information, and using descriptive details to elaborate on behaviors that seem familiar.

Score Point 1

Instructions Student Work and Commentary: "Hamster Care"

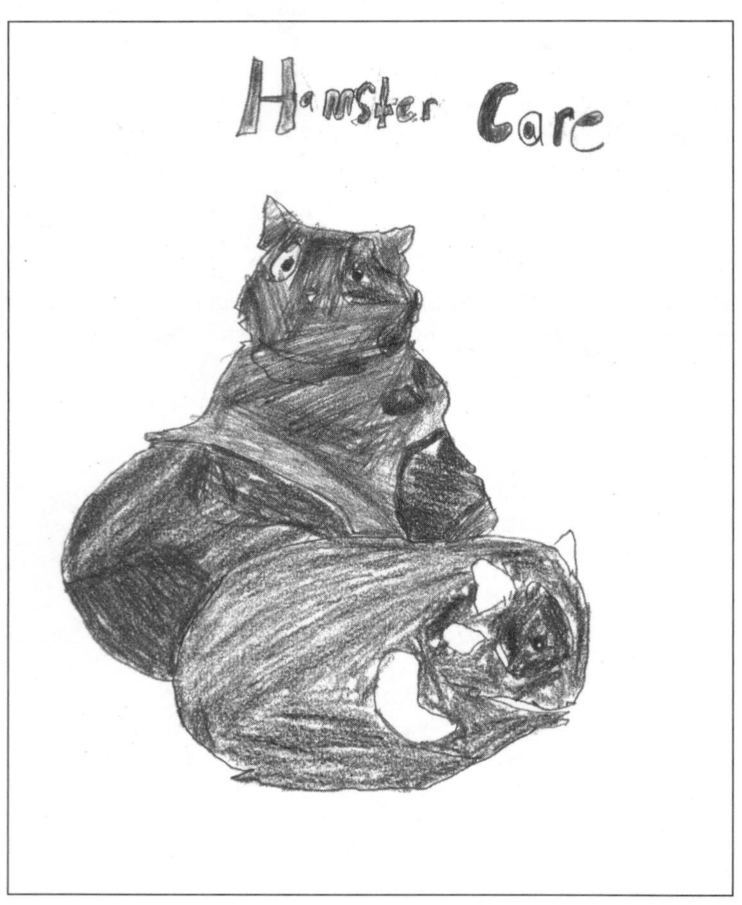

"Hamster Care" provides readers with a general series of steps related to buying and caring for hamsters. The writer provides some details about choosing a hamster, but does not elaborate on the different tasks involved in hamster care. In this piece, genre elements are missing or unformed. The writer will need substantial support to meet the standard for writing instructions.

The writer uses only the title to announce the topic to readers.

The writer attempts to engage the reader by expressing his feelings about hamsters ("if you love them like I do.").

The information about hamster care is divided into three general steps ("Step 1," "Step 2," and "Step 3: Hamsters like to play"). In Step 1, the writer describes the process of choosing a hamster. Step 2 describes what to do "If your hamster gets sick." In Step 3, the writer describes hamster play ("They can run up to eight miles on their exercise wheel.").

The writer provides readers with some details about choosing a hamster ("If a hamster has six dots it's a female. If it does not have any it's a male."), but there are many places in the piece where the writer provides few details or does not elaborate

Score Point 1 *continued*

step 1

First, you buy a hamster if you like them. like I do. If you want a male and a female, ask a clerk. They will tell you to follow them to the back of the store. He or she will show you how to tell a male from a female, and he orshe will tell you the difference. If ahamster has six dots it's a female. If it doesn't have any it's amale. If you already have a hamster cage thats good. If you don't you have to buy one. It costs about 19^{99} with built in toys.

on the actions he describes. For instance, in Step 2 the writer explains that a sick hamster should be fed "plane yogurt and children's Tylenol," but he does not talk about how to tell if a hamster is sick. Also, he includes information about what hamsters eat ("healthy food like oranges, carrots, apples, and hard corn"), but he does not say how much food to give hamsters or how often they should be fed.

The writer does not provide closure for readers.

The piece includes simple transition words ("First" and "then").

Score Point 1 *continued*

step2: If your hamster gets sick, give it plane yogurt and children's Tylenol. Give it healthy food like oranges, carrots, appiles, and hard corn.

step 3: Hamsters like to play.
Hamsters love to play. They like to climb on their cage. They can run up to eight miles on their exercise wheel. They will get tired after five mintes. Then they will start running agin.

Score Point 1 *continued*

Assessment Summary: "Hamster Care"

ELEMENTS		
	Needs Substantial Support	**Commentary**
Orientation and Context	• May announce the topic only with the title. • May attempt to establish a context. • May attempt to engage the reader.	The writer uses only the title to announce the topic to readers. The writer attempts to engage the reader by expressing his feelings about hamsters ("if you love them like I do.").
Organization and Development of Instructions	• Provides a very general series of steps (readers may have to infer some of the steps). • May not organize the steps or actions sequentially. • Provides few details to help the reader understand the instructions. • Provides little or no elaboration on actions. • Typically does not anticipate a reader's need for information.	The information about hamster care is divided into three general steps ("Step 1," "Step 2," and "Step 3: Hamsters like to play"). In Step 1, the writer describes the process of choosing a hamster. Step 2 describes what to do "If your hamster gets sick." In Step 3, the writer describes hamster play ("They can run up to eight miles on their exercise wheel."). The writer provides readers with some details about choosing a hamster ("If a hamster has six dots it's a female. If it does not have any it's a male."), but there are many places in the piece where the writer provides few details or does not elaborate on the actions he describes. For instance, in Step 2 the writer explains that a sick hamster should be fed "plane yogurt and children's Tylenol," but he does not talk about how to tell if a hamster is sick. Also, he includes information about what hamsters eat ("healthy food like oranges, carrots, apples, and hard corn"), but he does not say how much food to give hamsters or how often they should be fed.
Closure	• Provides closure.	The writer does not provide closure for readers.

Score Point 1 *continued*

STRATEGIES		
	Needs Substantial Support	**Commentary**
Transition Devices	• May use some simple transition words (e.g., first, now, then) or number the steps. • May attempt to use formatting to highlight specific categories of information or to signal transitions between steps.	The piece includes simple transition words ("First" and "then").
Other	• May use drawings or graphics to illustrate the instructions.	
Note: The commentary highlights the elements and strategies in the student paper, focusing on how well the paper addresses the totality of the elements and strategies rather than on whether each is included.		

Roadmap for Development

The writer will benefit from learning more about the genre elements of instructions. Perhaps he might benefit from reading instructions related to a familiar topic (for example, a favorite game) and talking about how those instructions give him the information he needs to play the game and also how they anticipate possible questions that readers might have. The writer will also benefit from learning strategies to develop fluency and stamina.

Response to Literature

The responding to literature genre assessed by New Standards is recognized and assessed in many districts and states throughout the United States, and like other genres, it provides a rough template that defines expectations for a particular kind of writing. But it is important to note that it is only one of several ways that readers and writers respond to literature and only one of several encouraged by teachers in school. Responding to literature can take many different forms. All of them are valuable in a language arts curriculum.

Students may respond in writing to literature in a variety of ways and for a variety of purposes: to express their emotional reactions, clarify their thinking or attitudes, explore difficulties in their understanding, or simply to share their opinions with others to build a social relationship. Teachers sometimes design classroom activities that invite informal, imaginative responses wherein the focus is on helping children make connections to their own experiences and to other texts or authors they have read. Such connections deepen children's understanding.

In the classroom, the development of more formal responses is supported both by these kinds of activities and by Accountable Talk[SM]. Accountable Talk offers a set of tools for helping teachers lead academically productive group discussions. Accountable Talk is not empty chatter; it seriously responds to and further develops what others say, whether the talk occurs one-on-one, in small groups, or with the whole class. When they engage in Accountable Talk, students learn to introduce and ask for knowledge that is accurate and relevant to the text under discussion. They learn to use evidence from the text in ways that are appropriate and follow established norms of good reasoning.

Built on this kind of scaffolding, formal written responses require students to examine texts thoughtfully and to draw evidence from them to make assertions and substantiate arguments. A good response to literature is never built on unsupported opinion. Polished and crafted for an audience, effective papers in this genre always demonstrate a comprehensive understanding of the work, and they persuade readers to accept the writer's interpretation or evaluation of a work of literature by providing evidence.

The New Standards expectations for responding to literature in writing center on this more formal, school-based genre. In the world outside of school, this genre is realized in published reviews of books, poetry, short stories, or other texts. Reviews are judged for the writer's ability to craft effective and defensible commentary—a coherent analysis that is supported by evidence.

The New Standards expectations for student writers in the response to literature genre require that student writers provide an introduction, demonstrate an understanding of the work, advance an interpretation or evaluation, include details from the literature that support the writer's assertions, use a range of appropriate strategies, and provide closure. Supporting judgments with evidence from the text is at the heart of this genre.

Orientation and Context

There are many ways to introduce a response to a literary work, depending upon the writer's purpose, but introductions usually share some common elements. Context is typically provided, such as the subject of the literature, the identity of the author(s), and the title(s) of the work or works that will be discussed. The writer may also attempt to engage the reader's interest by suggesting a reason for the reader to want to read the literature or by using an attention-grabbing lead. Some writers articulate the main point of their response in the introduction.

Comprehension, Interpretation, and Evaluation of Literature

The core of a response is the writer's interpretation and evaluation of the literature. Successful writers of this genre make assertions about the work that focus on the important elements of the text. They demonstrate comprehension of the work and a good grasp of the significant ideas of the work or passages in the work. They advance judgments that are interpretive, analytic, evaluative, or reflective, dealing with ambiguities and complexities in the text(s). They deal with questions about motivation, causality, and implications. They typically comment on the author's use of stylistic devices and show an appreciation of the effects created. They make perceptive judgments about the literary quality of the work.

Effective writers of this genre illustrate their interpretations or evaluations of the literature (for example, evaluations of an author's craft, interpretations of a work's theme) with examples or other information about the text. It is common for writers to summarize or paraphrase the work, or relevant parts of it, but successful writers of this genre do not simply retell. They make choices about what to tell the audience and what not to tell, depending upon the points they want to make.

Writers of this genre also sometimes compare and contrast the work they are responding to with other works that they have read or with their own life experiences. They may draw analogies between events or circumstances in literature and events or circumstances in their own lives. In other words, they connect the literature to their life experiences or culture. They support their interpretations or inferences by explaining the characters' motives or the causes of events based on their understanding of people and life in general. They often use quotations to explain and support their interpretation or to illustrate aspects of the author's craft. Used appropriately, quotations add to the credibility of the writer's conclusions.

Evidence

When students write a formal response to literature, they make a judgment about something they have read or have heard read to them. This judgment can be evaluative ("I liked it because...") or it can be interpretive ("I think the author is saying..."). Successful writers of this genre develop credible arguments to support their judgments. Significantly, this genre requires students to go back into the text to support their evaluation or interpretation. Although reader-response approaches stress the value of individual and unique encounters with text, reader-response theorists do not advocate the idea that every reading of a text is as good as any other. Louise Rosenblatt (1968) says that we must challenge students to be disciplined in the way they work with texts by (1) showing what in the text justifies their response and (2) making clear the criteria or standards of evaluation that they are using.

Because the deep structure of response to literature is argument, usually more than one assertion is put forward, and each is supported by evidence. Individual assertions add weight to the argument and relate back to the writer's overall interpretation or evaluation of the text. In order to make sense of the writer's interpretation or evaluation of a text, the audience needs adequate evidence—examples, details, quotations—along with explanations and reasons. Successful writers of this genre support their interpretations, inferences, and conclusions by referring to the text, other works, other authors, or to personal knowledge. They move beyond purely associative or emotional connections between the literature and their own experience (text-to-self connections) to explain how the connections they write about support their interpretations and evaluations. They convince the reader through logic and with evidence that is both sufficient and relevant. They typically use connecting words associated with reasoning (because, so, the first reason). If they are comparing works, they make accurate and perceptive observations of the similarities and differences between the works, and they support their observations by referring to the texts.

Successful writers of this genre express their feelings and reactions, but they do not overly rely on appeals to emotions or overstate their case. Although young children may often exaggerate or make sweeping generalizations, as they mature, their arguments are more often based on logic and reasoning. Successful writers of this genre do not make hasty generalizations marked by words like "all," "ever," "always," and "never." They qualify their claims, using words like "most," "many," "usually," and "seldom," when such words would be more accurate, and they support their opinions with evidence.

Closure

Although a response to literature may not always have a formal conclusion, writers typically provide some sort of closure, such as a summing up of the writer's perspective on the work. Writers of this genre often leave the reader with a fresh insight, a quotation, or some other memorable impression.

Response to Literature in Fifth Grade

Student writers at fifth grade show a growing mastery of the response to literature genre and of techniques for writing it. Many of them are able to produce well-developed and highly detailed responses. Nevertheless, within any single class, student performance may vary widely. Some less able students, especially those who struggle with writing, may mistakenly use the title or author of the text as the introduction. Others may fail to introduce the topic altogether. Less able writers, especially those who need substantial support, may comment on the text without providing the information that the reader would need to understand the comment ("I think all who are mean like Mr. Hazell and treat children badly like Mr. Hazell threatening Danny are evil."). That is, they may write as if they assume the reader already knows the storyline or the characters. The information they do provide may be scant and they may appear to focus on random pieces of information. These less able writers provide minimal evidence for their assertions, and the lack of detail in their writing may make it difficult for teachers to know whether they understand the story or not.

In contrast, writers who meet the standard at fifth grade typically demonstrate a comprehensive understanding of the text or texts they choose to discuss. They express opinions and make assertions about the meaning or quality of the works they read. They focus on the "big ideas" in the text ("Spindle's End tells how often there is a big difference between who we are and the role we are expected to play in life.") and they offer evidence for their assertions ("Both Rosie and Peony are stuck with roles that don't fit them."). Their summaries are detailed and their texts are generally well organized and coherent. They actively employ a variety of techniques to attempt to engage the reader's interest, such as quoting an intriguing piece of dialogue ("'But I can't—' Peone said, as she began to understand what had happened..."), previewing the problem and hinting at the resolution ("This book is about two best friends who try to stay close to each other even though one of them moves away."), or making claims about an author ("Roald Dahl is a very interesting author...because he knows what a kid wants to hear.").

In summary, students who meet the standard at fifth grade have a broad repertoire of strategies for writing about literature. In addition, their syntax and vocabulary are often more complex than the vocabulary and syntax of writers who do not meet the standard. Their sentence structure and vocabulary reflect a developing proficiency with written text and a deepening understanding of language.

Response to Literature Rubrics Elements

	5 Exceeds Standard*	4 Meets Standard
Orientation and Context	• Introduces the topic. • Engages the reader and develops reader interest. • Conveys a knowledgeable stance.	• Introduces the topic. • Engages the reader and develops reader interest. • Conveys a knowledgeable stance.
Comprehension, Interpretation, and Evaluation of Literature	• Demonstrates a comprehensive understanding of the work(s). • Focuses on the "big ideas." • Makes assertions about the meaning or quality of the work(s) that focus on the important elements of the work(s). • Presents an interpretation or evaluation in a well-organized and coherent manner.	• Demonstrates a comprehensive understanding of the work(s). • Focuses on the "big ideas." • Makes assertions about the meaning or quality of the work(s) that focus on the important elements of the work(s). • Presents an interpretation or evaluation in a well-organized and coherent manner.
Evidence	• Provides specific evidence from the work that supports the interpretation or evaluation. • Summary, if present, includes essential details and supports the student's assertions about the work(s). • Quotations, if present, support the interpretation or evaluation.	• Provides specific evidence from the work that supports the interpretation or evaluation. • Summary, if present, includes essential details and supports the student's assertions about the work(s). • Quotations, if present, support the interpretation or evaluation.
Closure	• Provides closure.	• Provides closure.

*The criteria that define score points 5 and 4 are identical. This is intentional. What distinguishes a 5 from a 4 is not the presence or absence of a particular element or strategy. Rather, it is the overall quality of execution and the level of language the writer employs. Writers of score point 5 papers bring something to the text that may not be provided by instruction—a deep understanding or passion for the topic and the genre.

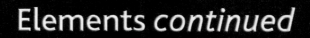

Elements *continued*

	3 Needs Revision	2 Needs Instruction	1 Needs Substantial Support
Orientation and Context	• Introduces the topic. • Engages the reader and develops reader interest. • Conveys a knowledgeable stance.	• Attempts to engage the reader when introducing the topic.	• May mistakenly use the title of the text as an introduction.
Comprehension, Interpretation, and Evaluation of Literature	• Demonstrates a literal understanding of the work(s). • May focus on "big ideas." • Makes assertions about the meaning or quality of the work(s) or parts of the work. • May produce writing with some gaps in coherence.	• May demonstrate a literal understanding of parts of the work(s). • May express opinions about the meaning or quality of the work(s). • May focus on random pieces of information. • May produce writing with gaps in coherence.	• May demonstrate a literal understanding of parts of the work(s). • May express opinions about the meaning or quality of the work(s). • Typically focuses on random pieces of information. • Produces writing that may lack coherence.
Evidence	• Summary, if present, may support assertions about the work. • Provides some evidence from the work to support the interpretation or comparison. • May present evidence without any accompanying discussion to explain its significance. • Quotations, if present, may support the interpretation or evaluation.	• Summary, if present, typically does not support assertions about the work. • Provides minimal evidence from the work to support assertions. • May attempt to use and interpret quotations from the work(s).	• Summary, if present, typically does not support assertions about the work. • Provides minimal evidence from the work to support assertions. • Typically does not include quotations from the work(s).
Closure	• Provides closure.	• Typically provides closure.	• May provide closure.

Response to Literature Rubrics Strategies

	5 Exceeds Standard*	4 Meets Standard
Compare/Contrast	• If discussing two or more works, focuses on genre elements that the works have in common (e.g., "They all have the same setting.") and provides examples. • May note similarities or differences between the work(s) and own experiences.	• If discussing two or more works, focuses on genre elements that the works have in common (e.g., "They all have the same setting.") and provides examples. • May note similarities or differences between the work(s) and own experiences.
Other	• May use knowledge of literary techniques or concepts (e.g., plot, theme, rhyme) to explain interpretation or evaluation.	• May use knowledge of literary techniques or concepts (e.g., plot, theme, rhyme) to explain interpretation or evaluation.

	3 Needs Revision	2 Needs Instruction	1 Needs Substantial Support
Compare/Contrast	• If discussing two or more works, may focus on genre elements that works have in common in a very general way with little supporting evidence. • May note similarities or differences between the work(s) and own experiences.	• If discussing two or more works, may make comparisons unsupported by reference to the work(s). • May note incidental similarities or differences between the work(s) and own experiences.	• If discussing two or more works, may make comparisons unsupported by reference to the work(s). • May note incidental similarities or differences between the work(s) and own experiences.
Other	• May mention literary techniques or concepts (e.g., plot, theme, rhyme).	• May mention literary techniques or concepts (e.g., plot, theme, rhyme).	• May mention literary techniques or concepts (e.g., plot, theme, rhyme).

*The criteria that define score points 5 and 4 are identical. This is intentional. What distinguishes a 5 from a 4 is not the presence or absence of a particular element or strategy. Rather, it is the overall quality of execution and the level of language the writer employs. Writers of score point 5 papers bring something to the text that may not be provided by instruction—a deep understanding or passion for the topic and the genre.

Score Point 5

Response to Literature
Student Work and Commentary: "Spindle's End"

Spindle's End

" 'But I can't—' Peony said, as she began to understand what had happened. 'But I'm *not*—'

'Neither am I,' said Rosie, through her own tears. 'I'm *really* not. I wasn't, even when I was supposed to be. I just *wasn't*.' "

Spindle's End by Robin Mckinley is the basic Sleeping Beauty tale. Except it isn't. Because Rosie who was born the princess isn't the princess, she's a village girl. And her best friend, Peony, is more like the princess or who the princess is *supposed* to be, than Rosie.

There are two major conflicts in *Spindle's End*. The first is obvious. Pernicia, a wicked fairy, having been defeated by the country's last queen, makes her revenge and curses the princess and basically the whole country. Then there's Rosie who is supposed to be the princess who really isn't.

The story starts out with Katriona, a young fairy with the talent of beast speech, being invited to the name day of the newly born princess. She arrives safely, but before the 21st god-parent give his gift, Pernicia appears. She curses the princess with her new & improved curse, and leaves. Katriona runs up to the cradle, and tells the princess that she can have her gift of talking to animals. The queen's fairy says to take the princess and raise her as if she was hers. So Katriona flees with the princess. Once she gets back to her village, Aunt who lives with her, takes them inside. They decide to call the princess Rosie. She would be explained as a niece of Aunt's.

Rosie proves to be a strong willed and intelligent young woman. She befriends the village blacksmith, Narl, who "everyone's a little afraid of," and he teaches her horse-doctoring. She begins talking to animals. All this time she lives with Aunt and Katriona in a cottage isolated from the rest of the village. But Katriona marries Barter, the wheelwright, and the whole family moves into his house which is a neighbor to the wainwright's house, where Peony lives.

Peony is the ideal maiden, sweet, helpful, considerate, pretty, understanding, and so on. Although Rosie and Peony had never really met, she made Rosie sick. She avoids her, but when you live next to someone it's hard to avoid them. When the inevitable meeting comes, Peony who knows she's going to say something wrong says it, Rosie tells her to "Get dead," and Peony falls down laughing, glad to have gotten it over with. Rosie laughs too, and they begin forming the kind of friendship that goes beyond sisterhood, the kind that helps shape lives.

A few months before Rosie's 21st birthday Igor, the 21st fairy godparent, knocks on door, comes in, and tells everyone there that Rosie is the princess, and they must find a way to protect her; keep her safe. Peony bursts in. She realizes what this means, and gets an idea. Igor looking at her has the same idea. They decide they'll pretend Peony is the princess, and bind the girls so closely together that they might cast the same shadow.

The two girls spend the three months until the princess's birthday in a tower suite at Woodwind, the closest noble's residence. A few hours into the party for the princess's birthday Rosie sees Pernicia appear. She has a spinning wheel with her. Then Peony rushes forth and pricks *her* finger on the spindle. Everything goes dark.

"Spindle's End" is a well-developed and highly detailed response to literature that exceeds the standard at fifth grade. This writer clearly articulates her interpretation of the text, and she supports her interpretation with evidence.

The writer immediately engages the reader's interest by quoting an intriguing piece of dialogue from the text ("'But I can't—' Peony said, as she began to understand what had happened. 'But I'm not—' 'Neither am I,' said Rosie, through her own tears. 'I'm really not. I wasn't, even when I was supposed to be. I just wasn't.'").

She establishes a context and conveys a knowledgeable stance by identifying the adapted version of the folktale "genre" on which the tale she responds to is based ("the basic Sleeping Beauty tale. Except it isn't."). She also suggests tantalizing potential answers to the questions raised by the dialogue as well as the irony that is at the center of the tale ("Because Rosie who was born the princess isn't the princess, she's a village girl. And her best friend, Peony, is more like the princess or who the princess is supposed to be, than Rosie.").

The writer then provides a detailed summary of the tale; in the process, she demonstrates her comprehensive understanding of it. She identifies "two major conflicts" in the text ("The first is obvious. Pernicia, a wicked fairy, having been defeated by the country's last

Score Point 5 *continued*

Rose is awakened by Narl. She learns from him that everyone else is asleep, he isn't because he's a fairy smith, and Pernicia took Peony with her. They find their way out, gathering a small army animals that had woken up.

They find themselves in a wasteland with a tall castle at the center. After the animals defeat Pernicia's creatures with some of Narl's magic, they pull the castle down using a rope spun by Rosie, and Pernicia comes out with Peony in her arms. Rosie rushes up to them. Pernicia stoops, but it takes her a long time, so Rosie with Peony gets back to Narl, slides up on a horse and rides back to Woodwold. Then Rose goes into the Great Hall to finally confront Pernicia. The wicked fairy appears and casually points her wand at Rosie. Rosie runs to her, and tries to strangle her. They go down in a tumble. Narl arrives, and sees that Rose is losing. A merryl, kept by a chain in the rafters, tells Narl that if he breaks the chain, it will do something. He does, and it flies up, and then falls on Pernicia. The earth swallows them, and people wake up. Because they still need to save Peony, Narl and some others flow power into Rosie, and she kisses her. The princessness goes into Peony, and she wakes up.

They continue the switch of places so that both girls can go to a life that suits them.

Because of their friendship, Peony and Rosie developed some of the same habits, but their personalities stayed different. Rosie is sort of roughly shy and doesn't say that much, and Peony who has great conversation skills unless she's in love. Rosie is very intelligent, determined and caring as she shows in this quote: " 'Fast,' said Rosie. 'Fast! Listen to me. You must walk. You've run too far, and all you're muscles are going to seize up on you. Fast, can you hear me?' " She is proud of who she is or who she has become, despite who she is supposed to be. "Rosie shook her head numbly. It was true what Pernicia said, that Rosie was not a princess, but she knew that already. She knew that Pernicia said it to hurt her, but it did not hurt her." Peony wants to be helpful to other people, but even more than that, she wants to be wanted. " 'And I'm helpful to them so it's not as bad as it might be—' " All in all Peony is much more of a princess than Rosie.

Spindle's End tells how often there is a big difference between who we are and the role we are expected to play in life. Both Rosie and Peony are stuck with roles that don't fit them. "Rosie said 'I don't want to be the princess,' and she could feel laughter and tears both struggling to get out." The role of the princess fits much better on Peony. When they switch places for good, you can tell that the author thinks that when you have a conflict between role and self, you should be true to your self. Rosie would have never been happy with the role of the princess, and it's perfect for Peony. " 'Lovely young woman, and clever with it. She'll make a splendid queen; she has all the right instincts and the grace to get what needs doing get done.' " When they switch places and are allowed to be themselves they both are happy, even though parting their separate ways is hard.

Being yourself is important. And even now when you can basically be whoever we want to be if you work hard, if the role you *want* in life doesn't fit who you are, then it's not the right role for you. If you can't be yourself and be the in role that you have, there's no way that you can be happy. So be yourself.

queen, makes her revenge and curses the princess and basically the whole country. Then there's Rosie who is supposed to be the princess who really isn't.").

The writer focuses on the "big ideas" in the tale—the differences that sometimes occur "between who we are and the role we are expected to play in life," and how to resolve those conflicts and "be true to yourself."

She uses examples and details to support her interpretation. For instance, she claims that Peony "is the ideal maiden," and she supports her assertion with details, saying she is "sweet, helpful, considerate, pretty, and so on." She also supports her assessments of characters with quotations from the texts ("Rosie is very intelligent, determined and caring as she shows in this quote: 'Fast,' said Rosie. 'Fast! Listen to me. You must walk. You've run too far, and all you're muscles are going to seize up on you. Fast, can you hear me?'").

The student supports her interpretation of the author's message that "when you have a conflict between role and self, you should be true to yourself" by pointing out, "When they switch places and are allowed to be themselves they both are happy." She explains, "Rosie would never have been happy with the role of the princess," and she uses a quote from the text to support her assertion that Peony is well suited for the role of royalty ("Lovely young woman, and clever with it. She'll make a splendid queen.").

The writer provides closure to the piece by giving readers advice based on the story's moral: "So be yourself."

Assessment Summary: "Spindle's End"

ELEMENTS		
	Exceeds Standard	**Commentary**
Orientation and Context	• Introduces the topic. • Engages the reader and develops reader interest. • Conveys a knowledgeable stance.	The writer immediately engages the reader's interest by quoting an intriguing piece of dialogue from the text ("'But I can't—' Peony said, as she began to understand what had happened. 'But I'm not—' 'Neither am I,' said Rosie, through her own tears. 'I'm really not. I wasn't, even when I was supposed to be. I just wasn't.'"). She establishes a context and conveys a knowledgeable stance by identifying the adapted version of the folktale "genre" on which the tale she responds to is based ("the basic Sleeping Beauty tale. Except it isn't."). She also suggests tantalizing potential answers to the questions raised by the dialogue as well as the irony that is at the center of the tale ("Because Rosie who was born the princess isn't the princess, she's a village girl. And her best friend, Peony, is more like the princess or who the princess is supposed to be, than Rosie.").
Comprehension, Interpretation, and Evaluation of Literature	• Demonstrates a comprehensive understanding of the work(s). • Focuses on the "big ideas." • Makes assertions about the meaning or quality of the work(s) that focus on the important elements of the work(s). • Presents an interpretation or evaluation in a well-organized and coherent manner.	The writer then provides a detailed summary of the tale; in the process, she demonstrates her comprehensive understanding of it. She identifies "two major conflicts" in the text ("The first is obvious. Pernicia, a wicked fairy, having been defeated by the country's last queen, makes her revenge and curses the princess and basically the whole country. Then there's Rosie who is supposed to be the princess who really isn't."). The writer focuses on the "big ideas" in the tale—the differences that sometimes occur "between who we are and the role we are expected to play in life," and how to resolve those conflicts and "be true to yourself."
Evidence	• Provides specific evidence from the work that supports the interpretation or evaluation. • Summary, if present, includes essential details and supports the student's assertions about the work(s). • Quotations, if present, support the interpretation or evaluation.	She uses examples and details to support her interpretation. For instance, she claims that Peony "is the ideal maiden," and she supports her assertion with details, saying she is "sweet, helpful, considerate, pretty, and so on." She also supports her assessments of characters with quotations from the texts ("Rosie is very intelligent, determined and caring as she shows in this quote: 'Fast,' said Rosie. 'Fast! Listen to me. You must walk. You've run too far, and all you're muscles are going to seize up on you. Fast, can you hear me?'"). The student supports her interpretation of the author's message that "when you have a conflict between role and self, you should be true to yourself" by pointing out, "When they switch places and are allowed to be themselves they both are happy." She explains, "Rosie would never have been happy with the role of the princess," and she uses a quote from the text to support her assertion that Peony is well-suited for the role of royalty ("Lovely young woman, and clever with it. She'll make a splendid queen.").
Closure	• Provides closure.	The writer provides closure to the piece by giving readers advice based on the story's moral: "So be yourself."

Score Point 5 *continued*

STRATEGIES		
	Exceeds Standard	**Commentary**
Compare/Contrast	• If discussing two or more works, focuses on genre elements that the works have in common (e.g., "They all have the same setting.") and provides examples. • May note similarities or differences between the work(s) and own experiences.	
Other	• May use knowledge of literary techniques or concepts (e.g., plot, theme, rhyme) to explain interpretation or evaluation.	She identifies the adapted version of the folktale "genre" on which the tale she responds to is based ("the basic Sleeping Beauty tale. Except it isn't.").
Note: The commentary highlights the elements and strategies in the student paper, focusing on how well the paper addresses the totality of the elements and strategies rather than on whether each is included.		

Score Point 4

Response to Literature Student Work and Commentary: "Author Response: Roald Dahl"

Author Response: Roald Dahl

Roald Dahl is a very interesting author to me. That's because he knows what a kid wants to hear. He has a "kid's mind". He is the only author that I know that makes up interesting words like Inkland, fizz wizard, and gobble funking. All his stories are the same type. I don't mean the same story written again and again. What I mean is that they all have imagination, made up words, and disgusting thoughts. Some of his stories that have those things are Charlie and the Chocolate Factory, Matilda, The Witches and Danny the Champion of the World. The Witches is the book that I am reading right now, and it is like The BFG, another book that is by Roald Dahl. They are alike because in The BFG, Sophie and the BFG, (the big friendly giant), are trying to stop other giants from eating human beings. The Witches has the same problem. The Boy, (he has no name), is trying to stop the witches from turning children into small

Because the writer of "Author Response: Roald Dahl" discusses several works by the same author, he does not provide a detailed summary of a text, a strategy frequently adopted by writers focusing on a single work. Instead, he notes similarities between the works, focusing on global elements that the works have in common. This piece meets the standard at fifth grade.

The author engages readers and develops reader interest by explaining why Roald Dahl is an interesting writer ("Roald Dahl is a very interesting author to me. That's because he knows what a kid wants to hear. He has a 'kid's mind.'"). The opening lines also make assertions about the quality of Dahl's works.

He establishes a context and conveys a knowledgeable stance by summarizing some of the literary elements in Dahl's books ("he makes up interesting words") and by including a list of the Dahl books he has read (such as *Charlie and the Chocolate Factory* and *Matilda*).

The writer's comparisons of global elements and the details he provides as evidence to support them indicate that he understands the basic stories in the two books he compares (*The Witches* and *The BFG*). He identifies global elements such as plot development ("Both stories have to stop evil people from doing something horrible.") and character development

Score Point 4 *continued*

> mice, and then killing the mice by stepping on them. Both stories have to stop evil people from doing something horrible. Roald Dahl uses a lot of similes. Some similes that he used that I like are: Up he shot again like a bullet in the barrel of a gun. And my favorite is: They were like a chorus of dentists' drills all grinding away together. In all of Roald Dahl's books, I have noticed that the plot or the main problem of the story is either someone killing someone else, or a kid having a bad life. But it is always about something terrible. All the characters that Roald Dahl ever made were probably fake characters. A few things that the main characters have in common are that they all are poor. None of them are rich. Another thing that they all have in common is that they either have to save the world, someone else, or themselves.

("A few things that the main characters have in common are that they are all poor. None of them are rich. Another thing that they all have in common is that they either have to save the world, someone else, or themselves.").

Unlike many young writers, the author explains why the evidence justifies the comparison. For instance, when he claims that *The Witches* and *The BFG* "are alike" and that the characters have "the same problem," he provides details from the two texts to support his claim ("because in The BFG, Sophie and the BFG, (the big friendly giant), are trying to stop other giants from eating human beings. The Witches has the same problem. The Boy, (he has no name), is trying to stop the witches from turning children into small mice, and then killing the mice by stepping on them."). He justifies his claim by explaining that the central action includes people stopping others from doing evil ("Both stories have to stop evil people from doing something horrible.").

The writer does not provide a summary sentence to close the piece. Instead, he closes by describing a final point of comparison between the texts.

The writer evaluates the author's craft and provides evidence to support his evaluation. For instance, he comments on Dahl's ability to twist words into a clever and creative new language. He claims that Dahl "has a 'kid's mind'" and supports his claim with examples of the kinds of fanciful and fantastic words a kid might make up ("Inkland, fizz wizard, and gobble funking").

The writer uses literary terms in the piece ("Dahl uses lots of similes.").

Assessment Summary: "Author Response: Roald Dahl"

ELEMENTS		
	Meets Standard	**Commentary**
Orientation and Context	• Introduces the topic. • Engages the reader and develops reader interest. • Conveys a knowledgeable stance.	The author engages readers and develops reader interest by explaining why Roald Dahl is an interesting writer ("Roald Dahl is a very interesting author to me. That's because he knows what a kid wants to hear. He has a 'kid's mind.'"). The opening lines also make assertions about the quality of Dahl's works. He establishes a context and conveys a knowledgeable stance by summarizing some of the literary elements in Dahl's books ("he makes up interesting words") and by including a list of the Dahl books he has read (such as *Charlie and the Chocolate Factory* and *Matilda*).
Comprehension, Interpretation, and Evaluation of Literature	• Demonstrates a comprehensive understanding of the work(s). • Focuses on the "big ideas." • Makes assertions about the meaning or quality of the work(s) that focus on the important elements of the work(s). • Presents an interpretation or evaluation in a well-organized and coherent manner.	The writer's comparisons of global elements and the details he provides as evidence to support them indicate that he understands the basic stories in the two books he compares (*The Witches* and *The BFG*). He identifies global elements such as plot development ("Both stories have to stop evil people from doing something horrible.") and character development ("A few things that the main characters have in common are that they are all poor. None of them are rich. Another thing that they all have in common is that they either have to save the world, someone else, or themselves.").
Evidence	• Provides specific evidence from the work that supports the interpretation or evaluation. • Summary, if present, includes essential details and supports the student's assertions about the work(s). • Quotations, if present, support the interpretation or evaluation.	Unlike many young writers, the author explains why the evidence justifies the comparison. For instance, when he claims that *The Witches* and *The BFG* "are alike" and that the characters have "the same problem," he provides details from the two texts to support his claim ("because in The BFG, Sophie and the BFG, (the big friendly giant), are trying to stop other giants from eating human beings. The Witches has the same problem. The Boy, (he has no name), is trying to stop the witches from turning children into small mice, and then killing the mice by stepping on them."). He justifies his claim by explaining that the central action includes people stopping others from doing evil ("Both stories have to stop evil people from doing something horrible."). Also, the writer evaluates the author's craft and provides evidence to support his evaluation. For instance, he comments on Dahl's ability to twist words into a clever and creative new language. He claims that Dahl "has a 'kid's mind'" and supports his claim with examples of the kinds of fanciful and fantastic words a kid might make up ("Inkland, fizz wizard, and gobble funking").
Closure	• Provides closure.	The writer does not provide a summary sentence to close the piece. Instead, he closes by describing a final point of comparison between the texts.

Score Point 4 *continued*

STRATEGIES		
	Meets Standard	**Commentary**
Compare/Contrast	• If discussing two or more works, focuses on genre elements that the works have in common (e.g., "They all have the same setting.") and provides examples. • May note similarities or differences between the work(s) and own experiences.	The writer compares global elements in *The Witches* and *The BFG* and provides evidence to support his assertions. (See Comprehension, Interpretation, and Evaluation of Literature commentary on previous page.)
Other	• May use knowledge of literary techniques or concepts (e.g., plot, theme, rhyme) to explain interpretation or evaluation.	The writer uses literary terms in the piece ("Dahl uses lots of similes.").
Note: The commentary highlights the elements and strategies in the student paper, focusing on how well the paper addresses the totality of the elements and strategies rather than on whether each is included.		

Score Point 3

Response to Literature Student Work and Commentary: "Reflections on Frost"

Reflections on Frost

"Two roads diverged in a yellow wood,
And sorry I could not travel both"
That is a part of a poem done by Robert Frost called "The Road Not Taken". Robert Frost is an incredible and powerful poet. He has the power to turn the world inside out , and to have you look at it in an incredible, different way!

Another reason Robert Frost is an incredible poet is he seems to make the poem jump out at you by using personification.
"Because it was grassy and wanted wear;"
is an example of really powerful personification. Personification means you can make inanimate objects have personalities.

Another strength is, he describes the woods he is in so well, like,
"In leaves no step had trodden black."
I felt I was in the poem looking at the same leaves.

Not only is Robert Frost a powerful writer, he also is able to leave the reader with an amazing message. In the poem, the character was making a difficult decision about what way to go at a fork in the road. This decision could change his life because of the different people he will meet and things he will see. I think it goes a lot deeper than just roads, like he is describing a choice in his life.
"Yet knowing how way leads on to way,
I doubted if I should ever come back."

Robert Frost is a phenomenal poet and in his poem everybody can make a connection. Like, have you ever had to make an important decision? I have, when I got lost in the grocery store! had to decide what aisle to take, like he had to decide which road to take.

"And that has made all the difference."

In "Reflections on Frost," the writer discusses Frost's famous poem, "The Road Not Taken." The writer makes an assertion about Frost in the opening paragraph ("Robert Frost is an incredible and powerful poet."), but she does not provide adequate evidence to support the statements she makes about the poem. This piece needs revision in order to meet the fifth-grade standard.

The writer effectively engages the reader and establishes a context for the piece by quoting the first two lines of Frost's poem in the introduction ("Two roads diverged in a yellow wood, / And sorry I could not travel both").

She introduces the topic and conveys a knowledgeable stance by making an assertion about the quality of Frost's work in her opening paragraph ("Robert Frost is an incredible and powerful poet."). This statement is the controlling idea for the piece.

The piece suggests that, at some level, the writer understands that the choice between diverging roads is a metaphor for a different kind of choice ("it goes

Score Point 3 *continued*

a lot deeper than roads, like he is describing a choice in his life."), but she explains the effect of that choice at a more or less literal level ("the decision could change his life because of the different people he meets and things he will see."). To elaborate on her interpretation, she compares the narrator's choice to a time when she chose the wrong aisle at the grocery store and got lost. The grocery store analogy suggests that she does not really understand the metaphor in Frost's poem—going down the wrong aisle in the store is not equivalent to an intentional choice between different paths in life.

Although she shows skill at organizing her text, the writer often presents evidence without an accompanying discussion. For instance, she claims that Frost "has the power to turn the world inside out, and to have you look at it in an incredible, different way," but she does not provide evidence to support that assertion. Also, she claims that Frost "seems to make the poem jump out at you by using personification," but she does not explain what she means by "make the poem jump out at you" or how personification creates this effect. Instead, she defines personification ("Personification means you can make inanimate objects have personalities."), and she provides an example ("because it was grassy and wanted wear").

The piece closes with the final sentences of the Frost poem ("And that has made all the difference."). Because the writer uses those lines to sum up the effects of her choice about aisles in the grocery store, the closing lines suggest that she does not have a comprehensive understanding of the poem.

Assessment Summary: "Reflections on Frost"

ELEMENTS		
	Needs Revision	**Commentary**
Orientation and Context	• Introduces the topic. • Engages the reader and develops reader interest. • Conveys a knowledgeable stance.	The writer effectively engages the reader and establishes a context for the piece by quoting the first two lines of Frost's poem in the introduction ("Two roads diverged in a yellow wood, And sorry I could not travel both"). She introduces the topic and conveys a knowledgeable stance by making an assertion about the quality of Frost's work in her opening paragraph ("Robert Frost is an incredible and powerful poet."). This statement is the controlling idea for the piece.
Comprehension, Interpretation, and Evaluation of Literature	• Demonstrates a literal understanding of the work(s). • May focus on "big ideas." • Makes assertions about the meaning or quality of the work(s) or parts of the work. • May produce writing with some gaps in coherence.	The piece suggests that, at some level, the writer understands that the choice between diverging roads is a metaphor for a different kind of choice ("it goes a lot deeper than roads, like he is describing a choice in his life."), but she explains the effect of that choice at a more or less literal level ("the decision could change his life because of the different people he meets and things he will see."). To elaborate on her interpretation, she compares the narrator's choice to a time when she chose the wrong aisle at the grocery store and got lost. The grocery store analogy suggests that she does not really understand the metaphor in Frost's poem—going down the wrong aisle in the store is not equivalent to an intentional choice between different paths in life.
Evidence	• Summary, if present, may support assertions about the work. • Provides some evidence from the work to support the interpretation or comparison. • May present evidence without any accompanying discussion to explain its significance. • Quotations, if present, may support the interpretation or evaluation.	Although she shows skill at organizing her text, the writer often presents evidence without an accompanying discussion. For instance, she claims that Frost "has the power to turn the world inside out, and to have you look at it in an incredible, different way," but she does not provide evidence to support that assertion. Also, she claims that Frost "seems to make the poem jump out at you by using personification," but she does not explain what she means by "make the poem jump out at you" or how personification creates this effect. Instead, she defines personification ("Personification means you can make inanimate objects have personalities."), and she provides an example ("because it was grassy and wanted wear").
Closure	• Provides closure.	The piece closes with the final sentences of the Frost poem ("And that has made all the difference."). Because the writer uses those lines to sum up the effects of her choice about aisles in the grocery store, the closing lines suggest that she does not have a comprehensive understanding of the poem.

Score Point 3 *continued*

STRATEGIES		
	Needs Revision	**Commentary**
Compare/Contrast	• If discussing two or more works, may focus on genre elements that works have in common in a very general way with little supporting evidence. • May note similarities or differences between the work(s) and own experiences.	
Other	• May mention literary techniques or concepts (e.g., plot, theme, rhyme).	She uses the term "personification" in the piece.
Note: The commentary highlights the elements and strategies in the student paper, focusing on how well the paper addresses the totality of the elements and strategies rather than on whether each is included.		

Possible Conference Topics

The writer will benefit from a conference to discuss supporting an interpretation with examples and evidence and being more explicit (for instance, explaining *why* Frost's language is so descriptive and how those words communicate an image for the writer).

Score Point 2

Response to Literature Student Work and Commentary: "The Marble Champ..."

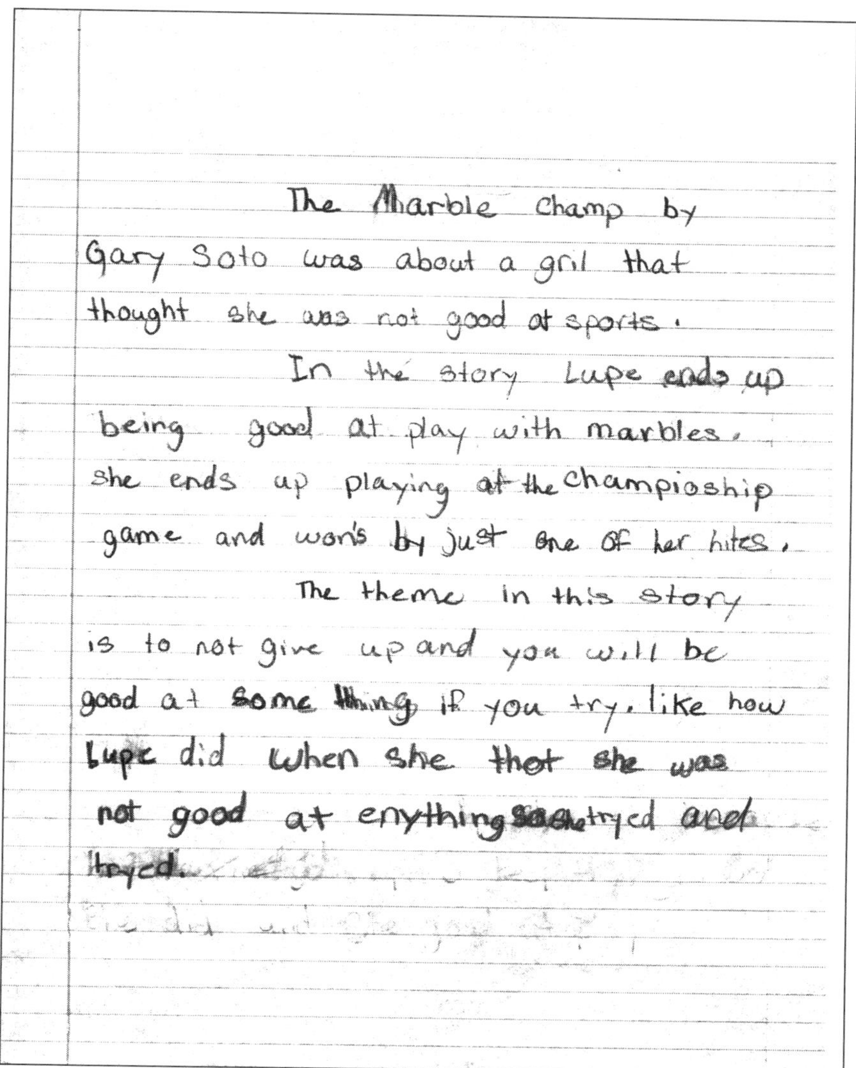

The Marble Champ by Gary Soto was about a gril that thought she was not good at sports.

In the story Lupe ends up being good at play with marbles. she ends up playing at the champioship game and won's by just one of her hites.

The theme in this story is to not give up and you will be good at some thing if you try. like how Lupe did when she thot she was not good at enything she tryed and tryed.

This response to *The Marble Champ* by Gary Soto suggests that the writer will need instruction in order to meet the standard. The writer offers only a general summary of the conclusion of *The Marble Champ*, and the piece is characterized by a lack of detail.

The writer attempts to engage the reader by announcing an important characteristic of the main character ("a girl that thought she was not good at sports").

The piece includes a two-sentence summary of the story that focuses on the story's conclusion ("In the story Lupe ends up being good at play with marbles. She ends up playing at the championship game and won's by just one of her hites."). He also offers his interpretation of the theme ("The theme in this story is not give up and you will be good at something if you try."), and he refers to events in the story to support his interpretation ("Like how Lupe did when she thot

Score Point 2 *continued*

she was not good at anything so she tryed and tryed."). The summary and interpretation are very general, as is the example from the text that he uses to support his interpretation.

The writer provides minimal detail about the character and plot development that lead to the conclusion he describes in his summary. For instance, he does not describe Lupe or her efforts to become good at playing marbles. In Soto's story, Lupe exercises and practices until she develops muscles and skills for playing marbles. Her parents encourage her new interest, and they even rig up lights in the backyard so that she can practice after dark. The piece does not discuss those important aspects of the story.

The piece does not include quotations from the text to support the writer's evaluations.

The writer concludes the piece by talking about the theme of Soto's story ("like how Lupe did when she thot she was not good at anything she tryed and tryed.").

Assessment Summary: "The Marble Champ..."

ELEMENTS		
	Needs Instruction	**Commentary**
Orientation and Context	• Attempts to engage the reader when introducing the topic.	The writer attempts to engage the reader by announcing an important characteristic of the main character ("a girl that thought she was not good at sports").
Comprehension, Interpretation, and Evaluation of Literature	• May demonstrate a literal understanding of parts of the work(s). • May express opinions about the meaning or quality of the work(s). • May focus on random pieces of information. • May produce writing with gaps in coherence.	The piece includes a two-sentence summary of the story that focuses on the story's conclusion ("In the story Lupe ends up being good at play with marbles. She ends up playing at the championship game and won's by just one of her hites."). He also offers his interpretation of the theme ("The theme in this story is not give up and you will be good at something if you try."), and he refers to events in the story to support his interpretation ("Like how Lupe did when she thot she was not good at anything so she tryed and tryed."). The summary and interpretation are very general, as is the example from the text that he uses to support his interpretation.
Evidence	• Summary, if present, typically does not support assertions about the work. • Provides minimal evidence from the work to support assertions. • May attempt to use and interpret quotations from the work(s).	The writer provides minimal detail about the character and plot development that lead to the conclusion he describes in his summary. For instance, he does not describe Lupe or her efforts to become good at playing marbles. In Soto's story, Lupe exercises and practices until she develops muscles and skills for playing marbles. Her parents encourage her new interest, and they even rig up lights in the back yard so that she can practice after dark. The piece does not discuss those important aspects of the story. The piece does not include quotations from the text to support the writer's evaluations.
Closure	• Typically provides closure.	The writer concludes the piece by talking about the theme of Soto's story ("like how Lupe did when she thot she was not good at anything she tryed and tryed.").
STRATEGIES		
	Needs Instruction	**Commentary**
Compare/ Contrast	• If discussing two or more works, may make comparisons unsupported by reference to the work(s). • May note incidental similarities or differences between the work(s) and own experiences.	
Other	• May mention literary techniques or concepts (e.g., plot, theme, rhyme).	

Note: The commentary highlights the elements and strategies in the student paper, focusing on how well the paper addresses the totality of the elements and strategies rather than on whether each is included.

Next Steps in Instruction

The writer will benefit from instruction on writing a summary that demonstrates an understanding of the text by communicating the main ideas and important details in the work, as well as supporting interpretations with relevant details and examples.

Score Point 1

Response to Literature Student Work and Commentary: "Danny Champion Of the world!!!"

Danny Champion Of the world!!!

I think all who are mean like Mr. Hazell and treat children badly like Mr. Hazell threatening Danny are evil, and he must be punished. Danny is a scruffy, adventrous little boy. He is an only child and has a caring, loving father. Danny's dad is a single parent, an automobile mechanic, and owns his own filling station. Mr. Hazell is a chubby, greedy, cruel, and a overeactive man. Mr. Hazell is trying to take over Danny and his dad's land. Then Danny has a stroke of brilliance and tries to poach all Mr. Hazell's pheasants.

In the end Mr. Hazell doesn't get his pheasants back. Then Doctor Spencer had a gift, he got six pheasants that didn't fly away. He gave two birds to Mrs. Clipstone, two pheasants to Sargent Samways, and two pheasants to Danny and his dad. Then everybody left. Danny's father wanted to get a new oven to roast the two pheasants and invite Mr. and Mrs. Spencer to eat with us.

THE END

The writer of "Danny Champion Of the world!!!" will need substantial support to meet the standard. Although he provides a summary of the book to which he is responding, the summary is scant and incomplete. Important details about the plot and the characters are left out.

The writer relies on the title of book to introduce the topic to readers.

The writer demonstrates a very general understanding of the "gist" of this book, but he does not include details that are important in understanding it. In Dahl's story, Danny wakes up one evening to find his father missing. Hours later, his father returns, and Danny is shocked to discover that his father has a secret—he is a poacher, one in a long line of poachers in the family, as are most other citizens in the

Score Point 1 *continued*

community where he lives (including the sole police officer). Danny's father explains that at one time, "just about every man in our village" poached pheasants and that "they did it not only because they loved the sport but because they needed food for their families." He also explains that the excitement "gets into your blood and you can't give it up!" As the plot progresses, Danny and his father hatch a plan to poach all the pheasants from the woods when Mr. Hazell prepares to host the biggest shoot of the season.

This response to literature leaves out significant details about the plot (there is no mention of Danny's father's secret); about the characters (there is no mention of the close father–son relationship that drives the events in the story); and about the book's outcome ("then Danny had a stroke of brilliance and tries to poach all Mr. Hazell's pheasants.").

The writing lacks coherence. In the second paragraph, a number of new characters are introduced without explanation as to who they are or how they are significant to the story. Also, this piece begins with an unsupported assertion that is not revisited anywhere in the text (Mr. Hazell is evil and must be punished.).

The text ends with the phrase "THE END."

The writer does not mention literary techniques or concepts; he also does not quote from the book.

Assessment Summary: "Danny Champion Of the world!!!"

ELEMENTS		
	Needs Substantial Support	**Commentary**
Orientation and Context	• May mistakenly use the title of the text as an introduction.	The writer relies on the title of book to introduce the topic to readers.
Comprehension, Interpretation, and Evaluation of Literature	• May demonstrate a literal understanding of parts of the work(s). • May express opinions about the meaning or quality of the work(s). • Typically focuses on random pieces of information. • Produces writing that may lack coherence.	The writer demonstrates a very general understanding of the "gist" of this book, but he does not include details that are important in understanding it. Also, the writing lacks coherence. In the second paragraph, a number of new characters are introduced without explanation as to who they are or how they are significant to the story.
Evidence	• Summary, if present, typically does not support assertions about the work. • Provides minimal evidence from the work to support assertions. • Typically does not include quotations from the work(s).	In Dahl's story, Danny wakes up one evening to find his father missing. Hours later, his father returns, and Danny is shocked to discover that his father has a secret—he is a poacher, one in a long line of poachers in the family, as are most other citizens in the community where he lives (including the sole police officer). Danny's father explains that at one time, "just about every man in our village" poached pheasants and that "they did it not only because they loved the sport but because they needed food for their families." He also explains that the excitement "gets into your blood and you can't give it up!" As the plot progresses, Danny and his father hatch a plan to poach all the pheasants from the woods when Mr. Hazell prepares to host the biggest shoot of the season. This response to literature leaves out significant details about the plot (there is no mention of Danny's father's secret); about the characters (there is no mention of the close father-son relationship that drives the events in the story); and about the book's outcome ("then Danny had a stroke of brilliance and tries to poach all Mr. Hazell's pheasants."). Also, this piece begins with an unsupported assertion that is not revisited anywhere in the text (Mr. Hazell is evil and must be punished.). The writer does not quote from the book.
Closure	• May provide closure.	The text ends with the phrase "THE END."

Score Point 1 *continued*

STRATEGIES		
	Needs Substantial Support	**Commentary**
Compare/Contrast	• If discussing two or more works, may make comparisons unsupported by reference to the work(s). • May note incidental similarities or differences between the work(s) and own experiences.	
Other	• May mention literary techniques or concepts (e.g., plot, theme, rhyme).	The writer does not mention literary techniques or concepts.
Note: The commentary highlights the elements and strategies in the student paper, focusing on how well the paper addresses the totality of the elements and strategies rather than on whether each is included.		

Roadmap for Development

The lack of detail about the characters and key elements in the plot makes it difficult to know whether the writer of this response really understood the story as a whole. In order to write an effective response to literature, the student must have an understanding of the big events and main ideas in the book; the problems in this response may result from a reading issue. The writer also needs specific instruction about the genre elements for a response to literature, for example, making an assertion and supporting it with examples from the book. Using book reviews and blurbs as models might be one way to help this student become more familiar with the genre.

References

Black, P., & Wiliam, D. (1998). Inside the black box: Raising standards through classroom assessment. *Phi Delta Kappan*, *80*(2), 139–149.

Bruner, J. (1985). Narrative and paradigmatic modes of thought. In E. Eisner (Ed.), *Learning and teaching the ways of knowing* (pp. 97–115). Chicago: University of Chicago Press.

Cooper, C.R. (1999). What we know about genres, and how it can help us assign and evaluate writing. In C.R. Cooper & L. Odell (Eds.), *Evaluating writing: The role of teachers' knowledge about text, learning, and culture* (pp. 23–52). Urbana, IL: National Council of Teachers of English.

Derewianka, B. (1990). *Exploring how texts work*. Newtown, Australia: Primary English Teaching Association.

Hillocks, G., Jr. (1984). What works in teaching composition: A meta-analysis of experimental treatment studies. *American Journal of Education*, *93*(1), 133–170.

Rosenblatt, L. (1968). A way of happening. *Educational Record*, *49*, 339–346.